The Alchemy Spoon
Issue 3: April 2021

The Alchemy Spoon
Issue 3: April 2021

Editors
Roger Bloor
Vanessa Lampert
Mary Mulholland

A poetry magazine with a special interest in 'new phase' poets

Design and production
Clayhanger Press

Typeset in Times New Roman

Poetry Submissions
Submission window next open from 1st – 30th June 2021

Please read the submissions guidelines on the final page
Submissions are through the website
www.alchemyspoon.org

Cover Images
Front Cover: *To the Whitechurch Graves* by Seán Kiely
Back Cover: *Invocation (2016)* by John Brennan

And I will show you something different from either
Your shadow at morning striding behind you
Or your shadow at evening rising to meet you;
I will show you fear in a handful of dust.

T.S.Eliot, *The Waste Land*

Contents

Editorial

A spell is concentrated poetry ~ F. McEachran [1]

The idea of poetry as 'spells' was used by F. McEachran, a teacher at Shrewsbury School and Shrewsbury Girls High School in the 1960s, to explain the system he employed with his pupils to enable them to experience the joy of chanting poetry in chorus. He believed that, in addition to inducing a sense of joy, chanting poems also let the pupils distinguish between what he termed 'the two kinds of impact on the human sensibility', the sonal or incantatory aspect, and the 'more traditional beauty' of poetry which arises from both content and structure. This was an idea echoed by Denise Levertov when she discussed the 'complex surfaces of denotive and conative meaning as well as of sound patterns' and challenged the wisdom of teaching methods that are based on the premise that poetry is a problem to be solved [2].

The etymology of 'spell' suggests a derivation from the meaning of 'tale' or 'recital', linked to the parallel meaning of an incantation and the clear associations with 'enchanted', through 'spellbound' and 'spellbinder'. There are also the distinctly separate meanings of spell as both the creation of words, the correct ordering of letters and the use of spell as a period of time.

The craft of poetry, the construction of 'small machines of words' [3] by the ordering of letters, the incantatory nature of poetry, the narrative strands that run through poetry and the changes over time in poetic form all justify McEachran's choice of 'spell' as a label for his teaching methods.

Edward Hirsch discusses the act of putting simple words in a rhythmical order to produce something of magical potency [4], quoting Christopher Smart's lines translated from Horace's *Art of Poetry*:

> It is exceedingly well
> To give a common word the spell
> To greet you as intirely new

This transformation of words through the alchemy of poetry breathes life into our machines of words and creates something which can produce an effect on the reader regardless of separation between the poet and the reader in time or space. All magical paradigms involve some form of action at a distance, whether that is distance in space or time or both. The ability of the poem to transmit and induce feelings at a distance was described by Rebecca Tamás and Sarah Shin as taking us into a realm where 'words can influence the universe' [5].

The craft of poetry is ultimately dependent on the art of transformation. In discussing the magical elements in Emily Dickinson's poetry Eleanor Heginbotham describes the work of poets

[1] F McEachran, *Spells* (Oxford: Basil Blackwell, 1953)

[2] Jewel Spears Brooker ed, *Conversations with Denise Levertov* (Jackson: University Press of Mississippi, 1998)

[3] William Carlos Williams, *Selected Essays of William Carlos Williams* (New York: New Directions,1969)

[4] Edward Hirsch, *How to Read a Poem and Fall in Love with Poetry* (New York: Mariner Books, 1999)

[5] Sarah Shin and Rebecca Tamás, Eds. *Spells: 21st-Century Occult Poetry* (Ignota Press, 2018)

in terms of magic: '...their enterprise depends on the condensed magic of metaphor and simile, of metonymy and synecdoche, of irony and allusion and personification.' [6]

The alchemy of poetry is undeniable. It takes the base metal of words and through craft and art transmutes them to a higher form, but the task of poet is even more complex, for the end product must also be invested with its own magic to allow it to transform the reader to alchemist. This is the nature of the spell the poem casts when it enables the reader to function as their own spellbinder.

The interpretations of 'Spell' by the poets who submitted work for this issue encompassed a number of the elements of magical connections, and many others besides. You will find a rich and varied selection of poetry within these pages, spells and potions intermingled with magical sparks of humour and insightful reviews.

The interview with Pascale Petit on page 57 explores some of the aspects of her creative method and sources of inspiration, containing valuable advice for 'new phase' poets: 'persevere, be tenacious as a bulldog', which I imagine could become a motto for all poets everywhere. Of course, if those are not working then a resort to magical intervention might be called for, and a suitable nostrum may be contained in Katherine Duffy's poem on page 20 'A Spell for Literary Success'.

Whilst the theme of 'Spell' has inevitably brought in a majority of poems with a magical or occult focus, our contributors have also explored the mysterious and often miraculous properties of cups of tea and glasses of whisky. They have taken us to the Appalachians to explore the mysteries of folk-wisdom and introduced us to strange and terrible things, not in the woodshed at Cold Comfort Farm, but in 'Ham House' and 'Box Room', New Orleans and Mexico.

The magic continues in a Personal View on page 53 in which Chris Hardy describes his experience of combining music and poetry, and we are pleased that his performing group LiTTLe MACHiNe have allowed us to use a video of one of their performances as our online reading for this issue, the link for this is on page 67. The idea of 'spell' as a key element of poetry is further examined in Lesley Sharpe's essay on page 64 which takes us deep into the world of magic and transformation that is found in the poetry of Adrienne Rich.

So, step inside and view the marvels of our poetic 'wunderkammer', our cabinet of curiosities, where else but within *The Alchemy Spoon* could you find such 'Exemplary Objects and Exceptional Images of the Entire World', a publication so full of poetry magic and mystery 'that One Could Also Rightly Call It a: Repository of marvelous things' [7]?

Roger Bloor

---

[6] Eleanor Elson Heginbotham, *Reading the Fascicles of Emily Dickinson* (Columbus: The Ohio State University Press, 2003)
[7] Samuel Quiccheberg, *Inscriptiones,* Translated from the 1565 publication by Mark A. Meadow and Bruce Robertson (Los Angeles: Getty Publications, 2013)

Dry Spell

Smoke rises across the plains –
an acrimonious whisper
of flames that licked through
valleys, incensed and
wind-swept

And the rains will come
drowning out the cries
of the mourning dove –

a last eulogy
to the voices heard in the fire

And all that will remain
aside from charred stone
upon the man-made troughs

will be the red earth
as it was meant to be
clinging to itself in
self-fulfilling
prophecy

Melody Wang

New Broom

It is not far-fetched to say there was at least a touch of it in our house, how she would never wear green or open an umbrella indoors, and if the Romani came she'd buy their heather, and spilt salt she always threw over one shoulder, or both for good measure. Apart from the occasional ladder or mirror, we lived well enough, crammed in a one-bedroom flat with two cats for company and the largest spiders you've ever seen. Good fortune followed my sister to America and me to a wandering life. My mother picked a four-leafed clover for a husband and that was her future decided. As for my grandmother, she was away with the fairies, taken in the middle of the night, and not a single speck of dust remained.

Pat Winslow

Secret language

How these gladwrapped old words become
something meaningful between us.
To anyone but you and I and your sister
they're drivel, seeming indecipherable since

we've complicated them enough, but we
come back to them today after the wake
with a sense of loss and excitement
like returning to the house that hosted the past

and finding it abandoned.
We lose our bearings but feel
the pass-the-parcel-joy of unpacking
this code. We work backwards: we must have

put a v before each a, a k before the os,
reversed these syllables.
And there's a ring to it now, a thrill,
like a key that fits, and we triumph

as if we had decoded the Voynich manuscript.
But what is it for?
Once we used it to badmouth
the man who reclined his seat all the way

back for an entire transatlantic flight,
or to tell each other that the boy to our left
had a freckle worth biting on his neck.
Or that summer, when we got a lot of practice

hiding those puppies in our room, taking turns
to go and feed them lest my mother see us,
which she had, of course.
But today it's just another way

of saying the same thing, and what's the use
of poetry if we can spell it out,
what's the point of my dead mother's cardigan
sitting in my drawer, and why don't we sell

our grandparents' decrepit cabin?
What are we holding on to?
A lost language rusticating in some neural grove?
A code for our coterie?

It's more, I know. It's a spell.
A spell of summer in the morbid hour,
a sanctum, a wand you aim
to name everything again from the start.

Vasiliki Albedo

A poem travels to Bordumsa

Father Thomas read my poem
And sent it to Sister Lucy who sent it
To Sister Mary who sent it

To Sister Stella who set it to tune.
She did not have a phone or lights on,
But she had a guitar voice

That lit up a thousand stars
In the moonlight.
There were crickets trilling in the dark

The sound of dung beetles, an odd croak
Of a frog, village fish in the pond that came up
From crystal waters to hear her sing.

The words didn't matter.
What remained was the feeling, something like
Joan Baez or Joni Mitchell, but better.

The song was carried by birds, flies, dung beetles,
Eagle, hawk and sparrow.
It found a place in the narrow space

Of the human heart. Backseat, a mountain jeep trundling down.
Father Thomas says the world is flat.
I think it means crickets are still dreaming.

Amlanjyoti Goswami

The Ways of Light

Fragments are sized, anchored,
and oiled by steady hands,

a knotted heart elongates –
as the map of long slow grain

reaches out across the afternoon,
where all that matters is the alchemy

of light and shadow, its path
across the mellowed wood.

Linda Ford

Der Blick

Ich weiß,
andere reden von
Lippen,
Herz,
Schoß.

Mir tun Genüge deine Augen.

Nicht Lockung,
noch Verheißung.
Sie sind mir
schon alles.

Der Blick,
der auf dich fällt
und den du mir zurückreichst,
lässt ungestillt
nichts.

Wilfried Schubert

Exchange

I know,
others speak of
lips,
heart,
thighs.

Your eyes satisfy me.

Neither enticement
nor promise:
already all.

My gaze
falls and you
hand it back to me,
leaving me wanting
nothing.

Wilfried Schubert (*translated by Moira Walsh*)

New Orleans, Louisiana, the Yellow Fever Epidemic, and Marie Laveau, 1878

(A Terzanelle)

In this ravaging, savage summer of Yellow Fever,
Madame Marie Laveau, voluptuous Voodoo Queen.
Cast healing febrile-curing spells, this deliverer.

Throughout New Orleans, woeful screams, horrid scenes:
black vomit, bleeding eyes and flame-saffron-yellow skin,
the work of Bronze John, that hellish, murderous fiend.

Rabble-rain ditches, fetid drains, bodies dead, unclean.
Marie's own child at home, dire-sick and nearly dead,
her burning flesh turning bright carotene.

In the midst of unmitigated, spine-chilling dread,
Marie, take out your healing gris gris bag
with its eyes of newt and spoiled fishhead,

your chicken feathers, the balls of stags.
In these dog-days of rain and the stench of harm,
Queen, save us from loss, from body bags.

Everywhere there's illness. Mosquitoes swarm
in this ravaging, savage summer of Yellow Fever.
Dance Madam with Zombie around your arm.
Cast curing, febrile spells, this deliverer.

Sue B. Walker

Spell for Summer

Just sit there for a spell, they said,
and I watched for some proper person
with a wand, a spangled cloak and pointy hat
to whisk away the silence, the waiting.

> *No one appeared in starlight*
> *or in swirls of darkness.*
> *No one turned up in twilight*
> *or in breaking half-light.*

Childlike, I might be spellbound still
had I not realised long ago
that an incantation I call my own
is at the intersection of time & trance…

as at dawn in midsummer when a wren
cracks mirrored darkness, shatters silence
with the thin wand of her cavernous beak:
splinters sky into a sillion shines of magic…

casting out gratuitous stars, night clouds, all
without the chanting of a single charm:
miles from any wishbone silence
in the clockwork now of summer sunrise.

Lizzie Ballagher

Hildegard's Remedy

Hildegard von Bingen, 1098–1179, uses the word 'viriditas' (greening) to convey the healing power of nature.

And when a man's mind is buried like coal under the earth,

tie round his head a cloth in which sit cooked grains of wheat.

And let the softened wheat carry to his disheartened mind

memory of warm bread, the comfort of a kitchen where love

holds the ladle, a field where poppies and mice exult in summer.

Then clouds will pass, darkness and delirium will be shot through

like thunder riddled by light, and when the cloth is unwound,

the man will smile for the first time in months, will pluck a blade

of grass taller than his hands, put it to his lips and make it sing.

Rosie Jackson

[For Severus]

Falcon, falcon,
fly swift as Cupid's dart,
fly swift as coursing hares,
Bring Severus' love to me.

Eagle, eagle,
you alone carry the sun
you alone can bear the burden,
bring my love to Severus.

Owl, owl,
you can hear my heart beats for Severus,
you can see my soul longs for Severus.
Listen to Severus, bring his words to me.

O Falcon, o eagle:
your claws are sharp as any dart,
your wings as fast as hunting hounds.
Should Severus' gaze fall on another,
should his heart beat for another,
Falcon, bring me her heart
Eagle, bring me his heart
and I will burn them both to ash.

Do it now, now, quickly, quickly.

Jennifer McGowan

A Spell for Literary Success

Write
my work is fresh lyrical supple profound, etc.
The choice of words is up to you. For example:
it has a music all its own. For example:
it draws a reader's gaze and plunders their heart

on a long thin strip of paper. Read it aloud three times with feeling, then roll it up
tight and place in a saucer of Creative Endeavour ™ oil. This beautiful blood-red oil
is a blend of bitter herbs and rare barks and is crafted by a powerful witch on Etsy.

Do not use the future tense. In order to make a reality
you must believe that things already are as you wish them to be.

Light a purple candle, breathe deeply, and chant
I am a poet, I am a poet, I am a poet, and so on, using a mala made of chalcedony.

Close your eyes and see prizes falling towards you like golden meteorites from a dark sky.
Be so convinced this is happening that you have to duck to protect your precious brain.

Visualise the literary world as a crowded market square. Your own stall is a strong,
elegant structure placed in a central spot. It brims with your wares: shovelfuls of life, twists
of travel, the rich weave of relationships, your lover's lashes, your father's old black bicycle.

Breathe over your poems.
With each breath they glow brighter,
just like a bellows, yes.
You are creating a glamour.

Make some poppets to represent editors.
To any editors reading this, please don't be afraid — this is white magic;
the pins will be used merely to correct your thought patterns
although I do advise using one with a special barb
for those who won't accept simultaneous submissions.

Leave your scroll in its saucer of oil out under the full moon for an entire night. In the morning,
bless it, then set it alight. Let it burn under the watchful green of the laurel tree in your garden.
A thorn of hope will sting your heart when you dig down to the roots to bury the ashes.

Katherine Duffy

Amphitrite

her aching spine heaves towards the tide
it's time   she jettisons moonbeams
along the tattered strand line

her little fish   her shifty mermen
beckon from the far side

she dusts crusted lips with salt
weaves flaming coral on her skull
utters incantation

its burning tongue twists her bones
flickers round her hollowed lids
she feels its molten undertow

how her golden scales start to glow
how sparks fly from frantic fins
how blood coruscates the sky

Sheila Lockhart

Ghirlanda delle streghe

*Inspired by a 19th century Tuscan witch garland, made of feathers
and displayed in the 'Spellbound' exhibition at the Ashmolean Museum in 2018*

I look east, watching a pink sun stain the wooded hills.
Swallows rise, swoop, whistle as I head along the track.

The bird in my hand stinks but there are no blood spills.
It lay there foxed, head-less, a fine offering for my sack.

A strong omen, finding a bird dead and ready; it thrills
me to know that fate approves, hands me what I lack,

tells me to act now before we end up suffering more ills.
Fire has raised our old barn; killed goats, burnt haystacks.

Enough is enough! Our neighbour has hexed us: he swills
his mouth in venom, spits, causes our stone walls to crack.

I will weave a grim garland, where plucked feather fills
tight loops: beauty will trap this beast. I have the knack.

Dorothy Burrows

still

give me a nose
for the sweetest malt barley

> *take it nut-brown*
> *steep till it sprouts*

let me mix and brew mash
and give life
to strong spirit

> *let mash murmur*
> *in the boiler*

let me know that thrumming
> *stilla   stillae*
> *stillarum*

a drop then drops
let it stream from the neck

aqua vitae
clear potent liquor
from father to son

let no excise man
find it

keep it hidden
underground

keep it from harm
as I would
my son

Bill Jenkinson

23

Lucky Harmon

Lucky Harmon, he's out of it.
No worries about tuition, no frost
on a windshield, no bar mitzvah, no a day
at the beach. No longer struts, dances,
sleeps, or opens the book *Around
the Corner* These are words, said
the teacher, this is a page words.
His book closed, ours are open. One day
a sea shell to my ear, I heard the sea.
I imagine he did, too, but can't ask him.
The silence of the dead is ours, only.
He can't cry in a waiting room,
or at a daughter's side as the doctor
tells her "Because of gangrene we
have to amputate your leg." Can't ride
a board in gulf waters with a dog, gamble,
drink, chase skirts. No longer behind
a bar or anywhere, he's out of it. Others
are upset and will be with you and me.
Free to give and take, upset and make
others smile. As if he's in prison (for life)
and we're outside prison walls, free
to drop everything and go one sunny noon
into a dark Lowes cinema, the one
on Fordham Road he once reclined in,
one of the audience. He loved an audience!
No longer will I hear him sing, see him
dance in amateur light in his bedroom
with the bed unmade. Lucky Harmon.
Never to have been born is best.
How is it good never to have been born?
What about those who are born, suffer only,
and die? All they know is suffering, a bad
deal, tragic fate. Reality. Auden wrote
"..could not hope for help and no help
came." Life's mystery is at my fingertips,
and yours. What I was looking for was here.
We opened *Around the Corner*. The teacher
said, Let's read the first sentence.

Peter Mladinic

Bell, Book and Candle

I tease it open, this crumple of paper loosed from my daughter's clenched fist
that still holds enough of her heat to sear my heart and quicken its beat, forcing me
to breathe, just breathe, while the script reveals itself. Red-margined, turquoise-ruled,
inked in black, its heading *WANTED BACK* is twice underlined, and beneath,
in schoolgirl-neat print: *Matching cherry lip gloss and varnish borrowed last term*
Beaded top and skinny jeans Kate lent you for Sophie's party (or £30 cash)
Jade's blue stone slide (the one in the shape of a butterfly from Accessorize)
Four names follow: *Sarah Dani Jade Kate*, each penned with practiced flourishes,
and finally what I think looks like a chi rho, until I see a kiss crossed through.
And I know this is a potent spell, cast in looping words that even un-mouthed
can drag a young girl into young girls' hell. And I know too, that for her
I would fly into their rooms as they slept, turn into boulders on their chests,
conjure boils for faces and necks, summon cellulite, spots and pus from piercings—
but what I do instead is burn the page, and in my head keep a list of their names.

Sharon Ashton

The Box Room

The greatest secrets are always hidden in the most unlikely places.
(Roald Dahl)

I collected bunches of rosebuds from the wallpaper
and carried armfuls of them into my dreams,

I wrote notes to fairies and stuffed them
into the ear of a lion through an unpicked seam,

I climbed to the top of the wardrobe and recited a spell
three times so I could fly around the lampshade,

I stepped onto an eiderdown raft and floated
down a willow brushed stream,

I willed the tallboy to don kingly armour
and guard the gates of my castle with a mighty sword,

I remember how each evening a sage conjured
words from approaching shadows, encouraged me

to stand on an old blanket box beneath the window
and watch for the subtle greening of spring.

Ilse Pedler

Magic Moments

Suddenly there was a cloud of pink smoke. You actually said *abracadabra*, and
revealed the missing Queen of Hearts, but there was no real magic, only
Power, calculating, emotionless, mechanical. Unveiling the secrets of a jaded, tired
magician, who finally hangs up their top hat in a derelict theatre, as you
Enveloped me with your coercive control. An illusion, with no skills. A trick anyone
could do, easily mistaking a rabbit out of a hat for
Love, or intense Like. Or mutual trust, or respect. But you were too busy sawing me in
half, and as the audience gasped, I reflected about
Lust, a devilish spell to break. A hex that fills your blood and mind. Fake flowers under
a black cloak. You performed your last trick and I finally waved my wand and
Severed you from the Magic Circle and made you and those doves completely disappear.
My finest trick.

Heather Moulson

Stinkhorn

Life is not all maraschino cherries;
the light does not cascade, through sugar-glass
in golden beams, to sweeten her dusty room,
and there is no royal-icing on her roof.
What good are gingerbread walls in Autumn,
when the rain plays a Baroque toccata
on the corrugated iron of your barn?

Among the gnarled thickets and tangled groves,
she clicks her single tooth at the sizzle
and spit of crow-fat, heating in the pan.
She squats upon a nest of besom twigs,
woven in the soil to hold her witch's eggs,
where she hopes to hatch a sturdy man,
who curls like a seed in her future.

She polishes a gilded cage that swings
on a ceiling chain; she checks the restraints
for his arms of bronze; strong, tender
and tasty as month-aged beef. He could
be lured, on paths, where no path leads,
nor mortal dares. So she bribes the birds
with crumbs and feeds the darkness stones.

It was delectable, when she tasted one before.
But he was only a young and tender shoot.
So she plants a little cutting, in the clay,
to propagate like wild onions, bluebells,
poison ivy, mandragora, and the mushroom
mold in the woodland loam. She flushes, hot
as an iron stove stoked with flaming hag-bones.

She steps; smouldering passion from the pyre.
'Poke your pale finger from the earth, my love,'
she calls. Some fly-bait burrows from the dirt;
she makes the best of her disappointment;
plucks him by his limply bedraggled stalk.
Her man screams like a mandrake, in the skillet,
with her cauldron-fire hissing in the rain.

Oliver Smith

Devil-black

A kettle of blue galls begins
to rumble,
its jawed larvae frantic
in the rising heat.

Steam fills the room, veils
the glass.

We hold our breath,
add honey, hemlock, vitriol.
Swirl and simmer
and still.

In the cool of evening
we slip the ink from its stew.

Bottled and corked,
its devil-black is dense enough
to block the sun.

Hunched over centuries,
you scribe your words.

Each time you rest your pen,
ghosts appear behind the skin.

Jane Lovell

The First Cup

When I was fourteen my mother insisted:
You must learn to drink tea. A peculiar demand
next to the usual imperatives of tidy your room,
be back before nine, be sure to eat more fruit.

Perplexed, I allowed her to mix the elixir for me,
in a cup from a dinner set received for her 21st –
a reminder that she had far more experience
in these things. She stretched out

for a brogue of a teapot, brown and practical,
scooped grounds of tea with a silver spoon
used only for this specific task, in full
comprehension of its significance. I inhaled

the sublime fragrance of russet leaves
as she poured water, left it to brew. Ruby red
swirls leapt from the spout, tiny leaves danced
then settled. Forgoing the milk, I lifted the cup

sip
sip
sip again,
unsure.

This would take practice.

When I asked why it mattered, she told me
to accept a cup of tea was an exercise in trust,
a moment to bond. Behind that rim, secrets
can flow, help can be sought, questions answered,

worries welcomed and dispelled. A magical
substance casting a spell of welfare, of collective
responsibility. Beyond an American Revolution
with ships, kings, taxation and representation,

but a quiet revolution, of comforting
whomsoever may need it the most.

Naomi Murcutt

30

'This morning, I murdered my grandma'

According to history, this is how President Franklin D. Roosevelt once
greeted each guest who came along to his White House reception.
He wanted to know if anyone listened to what he had to say.
Judging by this experiment, almost nobody did. Or if they did, they
took no account of it. But you have to bear in mind
that they may well have felt overawed at being
in the presence of a great man. They may have been dazzled
and disorientated too, by the southern heat and by all that highlighter-
white paint – the walls of the President's residence are not
intended to present to visitors as fortifications but they certainly veer
towards the ostentatious – that 'dare to stare back at me'
façade dazzling everyone in the vicinity like a perfect set
of supersize teeth. As for the guests, their heads were likely stuffed full
of the various cupcake niceties they wished to utter. They will have
spent the previous night rehearsing and re-rehearsing their greetings,
concerned to deliver them well, so that they could go back
from this bright, shining centre of the free world
to their faraway homes without loss of dignity.
Evidently, the only exception (last in line) was
the President of Bolivia. He leant forward conspiratorially.
'Well, well,' he whispered into the President's attentive ear,
'I expect she had it coming to her, didn't she?'

Tessa Strickland

Ham House witchcraft

At my feet in the kitchen garden, jackdaws
are after the crumbs my predecessor on the bench
has dropped on the gravel.

Six of them at one point
from the flock moving between the bare oaks
and new-dug plots - back and forth - and again.

I am still,
watching-restful, taking my breather.

A goth and her birds are never parted,
my daughter says, bringing me mint tea
and scattering the birds.

Later, a crow with white feathers fringing its wings
makes two passes in front of me, while I read
of medicinal plants used in the 17th century:

tansy for fevers and sores, wormwood for nausea
and loss of appetite.

If I were superstitious, he might signify.
I note genetic variation and diversity.

Kate Noakes

A Blessing to Leave With

for Jackie Trobia 2014

Perhaps this is a trick;
another way of teasing me.
    When I think of you,
and I do so often,

I admire your tenacity
which keeps us together,
just a little longer.

On that rainy afternoon,
we came quickly,
because time was short.

Waiting, you remembered
something I needed to know.
Then nodding, searched for
a blessing to leave with.

    I offered a smile…
and you took it.

Antoni Ooto

Appalachian Grimoire

In these hollers,
every Christian woman is spellbound.
Folk-wisdom is no different from other sorts of witchcraft —
except by name.

Granny's cabin is a curio
of incantations. March snow in a mason jar —
to pale skin reddened by July. Cider drunk from a cobalt cup —
elixir for a throbbing tooth. And the cure for warts?
Wrap a penny and milkweed in cheesecloth,
tie it against the skin.

Often there's no explanation for her magic.
Holding a candle to the flue on foggy days.
Hanging a cornhusk above every door.

Wasn't till I was older when I first asked,
starting with the acorns. They line her windowsill,
rising from the wood like a row of galls.

See, lightning's been known to boil the sap
of a full-grown oak till the bark explodes plumb off.
The tallest ones sizzle its tongue best.
It won't arc towards the seeds —
piss in its own well.

She cyphered me too —
why I walk the fencerow in winter,
its barbed wire the rusty seam between land and sky.

You can't help but love the barren trees, the short days.
You're a new-moon baby. Born into the world
at its darkest.

Lorrie Ness

Playdate on the moon

She says she'll freeze time, pause the world
with one whirl of her wand, leave us free

to move as we like. We'll lasso streams of bunting
around the moon's crescent, swing ourselves up

with the strength of Tarzan, cheer as friends arrive
by balloon. Stash Earth's gravity into pockets,

fling it like we're feeding ducks, enjoy
warm granules between toes, feast on hugs

and grown-up sized milkshakes served in wheelbarrows,
which we'll race each other in. Sit on the edge,

arms over shoulders, legs dangling as we peer
through the world's most powerful telescope

down onto vast, spilt colour. Point out tiny cars
scattered like stickle bricks, play hopscotch,

sign our names on rocks in our best cursive writing.
Suck on sherbet fountains, giggle at how

they set mouths alight, coat noses from a tipped
tube. Make volcanoes out of glitter, cartwheel

across the moon's surface, hold hands as we marvel
at the satellite's beauty, draw this moment on canvas,

gift it to each other and, just before the magic fades,
pocket our treasured art, hug one last time, zipline

down the bunting, rope taut like our cheeks,
through open windows, into toasty beds.

Chrissie Dreier

Shapeshifter

Now naked, she reads the pages of skin.
Her reflection sags, comforting like
the gentle rise and fall of breast
caressed by lovers long gone.

It is a decade since she looked,
truly looked at herself, each wrinkle
mole, spider-red-vein weaving away
on the contour of paper-flake skin.

A scatter of freckles settles on cheek.
Her face has gained the slapdash air
of Pollock's brush, the random swirl
of Van Gogh stars cast over the Rhone.

She hesitates, and for the first time
perceives me, dares to speak my name.
The pool of her eyes are wells.
Dig deep, I think, intrusion is short-lived.

I wait to pull the breath from her body,
eyes lock, sockets like magnets
and in the split of time she reads me,
knows how the story will end.

Kate Young

Circe

In quiet moments she lives upside down,
then loops the loop of her musical echo.
Its ostinato pattern on repeat. Repeat.

This violet headed girl with no rights,
must be a series of wrongs, a goof of teeth,
a ganglion with gun metal breath, a stray.

Watch how she holds her entirety
on the bony landmarks of her palms.
A man is no match for the witch.

He comes to her with all his belongings
to leave emptied, with no place to run
from the awful noise of her skin.

Mary R. Powell

Koguryo Dreams

The dog dances   in the ancient realm of Koguryo
    Sleep   Sleep now   my young one   my blade

The singer sings at the park
The student dreams at the library
    And I dream too   in Choson where the blades clash

The cats sleep   on the garden house roof
    And I sing   sing of rain spattering dripping through cracked tiles

      as the man and the woman danced

    I dance no more
    I sing at the library
        where the woman and the man
        sang

    Where the student   a far-off look in his eyes
    elbows on his textbook   dreams

    at the library

And the child sleeps in him
And the child dances
And the child dreams

Nicole Lee

38

Friend Request

Decades stagger by that long-play record
of an afternoon of coupling, copulating.
Pure energy vivid still. Your determination
to take something, despite my incompetence.
Pneumatic passion > lasting impression.

A generation since we kissed but memory
makes me salivate like a man who,
for the first time, bites into a rum-soaked,
chocolate-covered fig. Nothing ruined
but the bar set higher ever after.
I could eat a moist fig now!

And here you are, out the blue –
a colour that knows me – on my warm
laptop a lifetime later, a continent away,
at an apocalyptic time. Undiminished,
aged but edible. Way over there You;
here I … back then something
happened that still tastes sweet.

Allan Lake

Spells

(Irresistible magical influences)

1. The July hot spells took our breath away. Playing in an afternoon rain shower, cooling our bare feet in puddles on the dirt road, we wished for a wand and a spell to make these days last forever. Although I didn't, really. I liked school.

2. One thing I could always do was spell the words. I can remember only one test in fourth grade where I misspelled a word. I was devastated. Even now, affect and effect and there and their and they're and your and you're and not to mention the horrors of lie and lay give me a spell of palpitations. Good thing I didn't live where tyres and colours were in favour. I'd have no defence. I'd have needed a spell to cope, or additional labour.

3. To have the power to cast one spell, to have one wish come true, how to choose? You can't cheat and wish for three more spells or wishes. It has to be firm and finite. You also can't wish to go back in time and change an event. Time does not work that way, at least not yet. As kids, we don't see the big picture of ramifications, don't have wisdom to evaluate impacts of life-changing moments and choices. Are adults any better? Should I wish for a perfect memory, to be able to thumb back through the book of days and recall all I have learned? Maybe I should store away my one wish so that if I'm asked on the spot with twelve seconds to respond, I'll be ready.

4. When I was ten or so, we played a game that required each kid to pick one super-power they'd like to have. Everyone's had to be different. The power of invisibility was a popular one (evade parents, rob a bank) or x-ray vision (see through walls) but my choice was to be able to fly.

5. This was different from the rainy-day game where each one got to pick one item from each page of the Sears catalog. Delight in picking the most fashionable dresses; critical thinking required about which tool or appliance would be most beneficial to own. Kind of like the other game where we decided what items required for survival would fit in one suitcase.

6. My grandma never said, "Come in and sit a spell." I don't recall my grandma doing anything but moving with purpose. When she visited, she cooked, sewed, washed dishes, looked after kids. When we visited her, she took us to see historical forts, bought bushels of beans that we had to shell, carted us to Vacation Bible School to make popsicle stick bowls and memorize Bible verses. No recliner in front of the TV for this woman.

7. My grandma didn't practice voodoo love spells like Marie Laveau. Queen Marie – she demonstrated that a judicious use of voodoo could bring about important life changes. I don't know, though; somehow forcing someone to love you could come back to bite. Better just to be lovable from the start. No poking pins into dolls.

8. I do fly, sometimes at night, spellbound behind my eyelids. Held aloft by friendly breezes, doing backflips and twirls and corkscrews before arrowing off to limitless destinations. The nice thing about that space behind eyelids is that it is infinite, and not black, but full of expansive universes, the *apeiron, wuji, wuqiong*. You can't fly to the margins there because there are none. Just keep flying, floating, twinkling.

9. Let me spell it out for you: there isn't such a thing as magic, except there is.

Gurupreet K. Khalsa

witch marks

hurry home child– it's time to go
the sky is reaching down for you, full of snow
your mother's gone– cover up the marks she made
they're your circles now– touch them to be sure
all around the fire and the door

you knew one day
we had all her secrets and let her walk away
no need to fear the nights alone
you can feel the metal scratching stone

stay on here with me
folded up as tight as any mouse
I'll show you how to stop your breath and heart
and listen for the ticking underground
for in this house– in the dark–
I've seen things live for hours
without making any sound.

Caroline Hammond

Under a Spell of Shyness

She haunts the bedroom window every day,
her alter egos lost in dustbin bags;
she's now the only actor in a play
where nothing happens, every minute drags.
She fears a footstep right outside her door
of no-one going nowhere on the stairs
for refuge on a non-existent floor
where desperate people hide away their cares.
Her neighbour waits in vain for minor treats –
an unexpected letter or the chance
to spot a passing police car in the streets;
despair is too much effort in his trance.
Although divided only by a wall
a spell of shyness holds them in its thrall.

Jonathan Bradley

Incantation for Lost Love

Select Candle Colour
She remembers the soft flush
of cheeks from nervous excitement,
the purity of the white lilies.
But reignition needs strength
and depth. A red candle.

Dress the Candle with Oil
hers is infused with the perfume he loved.
Carve Names into the top half of the Candle.
She carves the word 'love',
not trusting her drawing of a heart
would be recognised. She cups it,
pouring energy towards it
after sticking seven thorns from
the red rosebush he'd planted.

Clear the Energy around the Candle.
A ring of salt to cleanse, a softly-rung bell.
She remembers first kisses,
how days became weeks, became years.
How much she wants to return
to sleep in his arms, to wake
to his eyes gazing into hers.
Say a small Prayer and Incant.
She whispers his name first.
Then lights the candle,
its dancing reminding her
of their first dance,
the rhythm becoming theirs,
his body igniting hers.

The flame stops dancing, it gutters, dips,
rises but fails again. She'd checked
for draughts, sheltered her spell.
But the candle stands, half-burnt.
She puddles on the hard, cold floor.

Emma Lee

44

Rough Sketch

never said he was her ideal cup
of Earl Grey: just invited him to stay

and nibble her cream-cheese
and smoked-salmon canapés

then wash them down with a glass
or three of Moët 2004

before trying-out her perfumed bed
then flattered him by saying

he really knew how to make love

so played him along while turning
a blind eye to the way he swigged

her chardonnay and chomped
even more of her canapés

while secretly sweeping his crumbs
under her Persian rug

that was until another
more her cup turned up

Geoffrey Winch

Witch in a Bottle

'Glass reputed to contain a witch' on display at the Pitt Rivers Museum

Nearly a hundred years
inside this glass womb,
its hourglass curves, swilled
with glucose, silver nitrate
to coat the ribs
so they'll never tarnish
and no-one can check
for that creeping bloom of breath
to see if she still lives.

Someone feared her enough
to filch the half-moon clippings
of her nails, knot-up
the strands from her brush,
one of the old spells –
a clutch of bent and rusted nails,
forced through the bottle's mouth –
to scour her eyes, her skin,

the belly of this vessel, a pond
in which her spider-weight
has been ducked a thousand times
in the urine of the one who bound her.

Let her out, there'll be a peck o' trouble.

In dreams, you turn feral,
blood-roar in your ears as you race
for the woods, tear out the wax plug
with your teeth
and she pours herself into you –
boneless and silvered as a genie.

Uncorked from sleep, you're spilling
at the brim with her wildness, her grief.

Victoria Gatehouse

46

In time

The first (and second and third) appearance of a girl's menstrual blood is interpreted as 'an opening to First Creation'; she now exists inside First Creation, constantly changing her form, and this fills her with strong n/om (lifeforce among the Ju/'hoan Bushmen). ~ Camilla Power

In time
making the animal passage in hands
taste of blue   resurfaces
bells on ankles engorge
appetite of weather

men dance women's seclusion

mother root harnesses water
la lengua   idioma   es agua fría aves

we drink into new—ancient order—

blood
                   water
                                          breast

familiarity of   breath

rain dances on rivers   the menstrual flow of earth

Amy Bobeda

Day of the Dead

Bones bounce as I cross the boundary, feel the change, weave into the underworld. Flesh peels away as I pedal further, cavernous holes appear in my skull. I have foreseen our wedding. Purple flower gripped in my gumless teeth, a white shroud hangs from my shoulders. My beloved has a cane and a black top hat. The streets are lined with flowers, candles and grim hombres chattering – *choose a kind man.* I taste tequila, the flesh of the worm in the base of my glass. I have been faithful to the white cross. A shadow man gave me a parcel as a reward but I was shocked at the contents. How can it be the same school blazer after thirty years? Yet, here I am, pedalling on this dusty Mexican road to marry a gentleman. Honest to his bare bones, trustworthy as the death rattle.

Juliette Lee

Bella

Listen
to the elms that whisper
spells into the wind
winding crow leg limbs
winter-stripped
to split the sky

Mephistophelian murmurings
witching walkers
haunting hikers
sortilege shaped and stretched
spun into sensation
and the omnipresent fear
of being watched

and look
strange markings
on the monolith

who put Bella in the wych elm?

Mary Senier

in another time

after Sappho's 'Six Fragments for Atthis'

someone will remember us
                    I say,
                    even in another time.

the tilted magic in unwinding stars;
all the same—let's leave it in the
                    dream
somewhere in between swallowing
violets and the salt-sea taste
left by a taken memory.

someone will remember us
                    I say,
                    even in another time.

her santan lips against mine
and the moonlight at the tips of
our fingers—
                    tell me one last time
how she grew wings to reach the sky
and tread clouds painted violet to
follow a voice that called her name

only for the sun to pluck her out
of some pocket in the sky and
send her feathers fluttering
into the sea.

Lerah Mae Barcenilla

forget me not

after Zhai Yongming's "#1 A Premonition [预感]"

dreams appear to know something of this—

the weight of dusk on your shoulders
and the tides that brought us together.

with the saltwater in my blood i heard
you calling

my name

(it took me a while,
i'm sorry. i'm here now.)

let it be known that i answer to

rainfall / jasmine / the sea

and the way your fingers held
the sky
like your crown,
your quicksilver smile
the shade of the moon.

how can i forget

Lerah Mae Barcenilla

pieces of peace

1. the sampaguita flowers that used to grow in white clusters just past the painted gates in the half-light of dawn.

2. falling asleep in the heat of worn sofas to the sound of static on the T.V and the buzz of radio in our grandmother's room.

3. the myths said the sun and the moon were siblings and when they fought for who got to rule the skies, the sun god accidentally blinded the moon goddess – to make amends, they decided to rule for half of the day.

4. the lost tales and dried flowers pressed inside flood-worn encyclopaedias lining the wooden shelves like staves in a song.

5. the Ibong Adarna, mythical flame-feathered bird, whose song entices Sleep herself, they said she still hides in the woods behind the yellow house – no-one hears her anymore.

6. the small, white butterflies swimming around the emerald springs, the one next to the green mountain with the face of a diwata.

7. they still talk about the stranger who visits the village sometimes. she glides through the lonely strip of road like a myth, eyes lingering too long on the gates. then she disappears. no-one knows her name.

8. the sun-yellow lansones sold by the side of the roads by strangers with familiar smiles.

9. no-one talks about the ones who disappear. they leave the scent of sampaguita in their wake.

10. it's all stories, really. just stories.

Lerah Mae Barcenilla

A Personal View

Chris Hardy looks back on a life spent in and around music and poetry.

I am a poet and guitar player and have always been greatly affected by song writers. I don't distinguish between songs and poems: they both use words, and many poems are also songs. Homer and Sappho sang and performed their work to music. To me, the 20th century blues musicians and those who learned from them and invented Rock & Roll, Rhythm & Blues etc. are great poets – Son House, John Hurt, Skip James, Robert Johnson, Howling Wolf, Big Bill Broonzy, Chuck Berry, Bob Dylan, Leonard Cohen and many others.

'I've got the key to the highway
I'm billed out and bound to go,
I'm going to leave here running because
walking is much too slow.'
(Big Bill Broonzy)

I was a professional musician, playing solo and in duos, influenced by Dylan, The Incredible String Band, Bert Jansch, James Taylor etc, together with folk blues players from the USA of the 20's – 50's, Brownie McGhee, Skip James, John Hurt and many others. I could have persisted with this – made a living of a sort as a session musician – and maybe the breaks would have come. But I became a teacher, and that's what I should have avoided, somehow.

Teaching is rewarding but intensely demanding. It has value – I worked in inner London schools for decades, and hopefully helped thousands of children from deprived backgrounds, and refugees and asylum seekers from war zones in Europe, Africa and the Middle East, to be able to live richer, happier lives. At first I thought I'd teach for a while, when we needed money quickly to pay rent, feed ourselves and our baby. But then I stayed – the salary is a terrible temptation and anchor. And once you get experience the job can be straightforward – you know what to do and can live round it. There's twelve weeks holiday a year (and I made sure those weeks were for music and travel). But it is exhausting and drains your nervous strength too. That saps the ability to write, and perform, though I somehow managed to continue with both.

I got out early, and since then LiTTLe MACHiNe has happened, together with collections of poetry and more poems. The members of LiTTLe MACHiNe (Steve Halliwell, Walter Wray and I) set famous poems to music. Usually one of us will bring an arrangement to a rehearsal and then the three of us will work together to form it into a piece of music to be performed live, and recorded. We want to help these great and famous poems escape from universities and classrooms, where they've been jailed on shelves, in books and syllabuses. We've performed to thousands of people and after hearing our settings of classics such as 'Adlestrop', 'The Lake Isle of Innisfree', or 'Ozymandias' they say, 'You've sent me back to the poems', 'The words sound even better like that', 'I wish we'd been taught poetry that way in school'. It's very pleasing that poets like Liz Berry, Carol Ann Duffy, Gillian Clark, Roger McGough and many others have encouraged us to set their writing to music.

I never thought of making money from poetry. I would rather not write to order, and never found the opportunity to write poems for a living. Few poets earn anything much from book sales. Also, to write poems you need to be exposed to ordinary life, be with people who are not interested in literature. To me the ideal poet's life would be Gary Snyder, working in the forests of North America, William Carlos Williams the doctor, or Byron and Shelley living by debt, adventure, fame. Matthew Arnold, Wallace Stevens, Yeats, Eliot, Ted Hughes and Larkin worked and wrote – their lives, work and poetry were connected rooms. 'You cup your hands/ and gulp from them the dailiness of life' (Randall Jarrell, 'Well Water').

I have had the privilege in LiTTLe MACHiNe of observing Carol Ann Duffy and Roger McGough over several years. They make a living from writing poetry, diligently promote poetry, going into schools, and encouraging aspiring poets who constantly approach them. They work hard, travelling day after day, meeting the demands of agents, publishers, and deadlines, going on stage for an hour or more to move and amuse a large audience, just with words. And they always carry a pen and notebook.

I practise guitar daily, to keep physically acquainted with the instrument. I do not 'practise' writing poems by writing. I try to be patient, wait, and be ready for the moment, which is also a mood, when I become aware that everything in the ordinary world is of interest and has mystery: it is inexplicably strange that we are here, like this. Then it takes a prompt: a word, an image, a memory, a line of verse, a phrase.

> 'Poetry lifts the veil from the hidden beauty of the world and makes familiar objects be as if they were not familiar' (Shelley, *A Defence of Poetry*).
> 'Intensity of mood is the one necessary condition in the poet' (Edward Thomas).
> 'Better silence than forgeries... I wait for poems' (Michael Longley).

Coleridge said there is, 'A well of the unconscious into which everything drops, and the act of creation is lowering the bucket and pulling up images and words that have hopefully undergone metamorphosis'. This suggests you must allow and trust the imagination to make from its material, what you have stored from memory, the phrasing and imagery of the poem, and reveal ideas, feelings, understandings that you did not know were there. 'Since the poet more often than not sits down to write about nothing, the content, subject matter, of the poem, rises to meet the words from below volition... It is not a wholly intended process and requires trust'. (Nick Laird).

I try to be in the right place, physically, mentally and emotionally, to allow poems to appear – healthy, alert, awake, waiting for a signal that switches on my attention – there's a poem there. Then enjoy discovering what the poem reveals, what I didn't know I knew, and feel cheerful there's a poem in a drawer, waiting to be attended to.

> 'Anything, however small, may make a poem. Nothing, however great, is certain to' (Edward Thomas).

I started writing when I was at boarding school, influenced by the Romantics, the War poets, the Elizabethans. The exam curriculum introduced me to poetry! I also had a couple of good English teachers. Reading Keats's Hyperion for 'A' level prompted me to start writing poetry. Mnemosyne, the muse of memory, appears in Keats's unfinished epic and my poem is a recollection of how all this came together.

Mnemosyne

Three plates of egg and chips
with tea.
A table covered in white cloth
near a window.
Afternoon light through glass
misted by steam.
The kitchen clattered by chat
and washing up.

Mick Coates, Charles Fry,
Hyperion.
Beneath the table write
short lines
for the first time down a page,
not showing them
or myself what the words
say.

This continued at Kent University where I read English and American Literature. Some of the staff were poets who encouraged us, commenting positively on our poems, which was charitable of them. They invited impressive personalities, such as Auden and Graves, to give lectures, judge poetry competitions, and attend seminars. Eventually I discovered the satisfaction of managing to finish poems that expressed things that were important to me. Publishing started when I came across poetry magazines in London, where I was working as a musician. I submitted poems and began to get published: *Stand* and *Poetry Review* were among the first to take my poems.

Some texts and authors I admire and which have affected me and my writing include: The King James Bible, Cranmer's *Book of Common Prayer*; Greek myth, *Gilgamesh*, Buddhist and Hindu writings, the Greek Anthology, 'Omar Khayyam', Thomas Hardy, Frost, Snyder, Ginsberg, Carlos Williams, Eliot, 'Cathay', Larkin, Plath, Bishop, Jack Gilbert, Philip Levine, Cavafy, Seferis, DH Lawrence, Raymond Carver and Arun Kolatkar.

Poetry seems popular and available, but its impact on national culture, in the media, is limited: there is little Arts Council funding, publishing concentrates on other forms of literature, and poetry has nothing like the impact of the music industry. But nothing beats finding a poem, finishing it and seeing it go off into the world on its own.

There's no money or fame in it, but when something needs saying the public, and the State, turn to poetry (and music) – funerals, weddings, remembering war, resisting violence. It is uniquely able to express profound feelings and ideas and measure up to such moments.

'I once more smell the dew and rain and relish versing'. (George Herbert)

Chris Hardy

Other works by Chris Hardy include:

Poetry:
Buddha (Holt, Rinehart and Wilson, 1984)
Swimming In The Deep (Diamond Mine –Hub Editions, 2002)
A Moment Of Attention (Original Plus, 2008)
Write Me A Few Of Your Lines (Graft Poetry, 2012)
Sunshine At The End Of The World (Indigo Dreams Publishing, 2017)

Music:
Health To Your Hands (Spiderfinger Records, 2010)

With LiTTLe MACHiNe:
MADAM LIFE (2010), *A BLACKBIRD SANG* (2014), *FRABJOUS DAY* (2018)
all Hotel Zulu records. www.little-machine.com

The Interview

Pascale Petit is a major prizewinning poet and beloved mentor of many. *The Zoo Father*, about her father's abuse, and three further collections were shortlisted for the TS Eliot. *Mama Amazonica*, about her mother's mental illness, won the RSL Ondaatje Prize and Laurel Prize. Her latest collection, *Tiger Girl*, about her Indian grandmother, was shortlisted for the 2020 Forward Prize. Mary Mulholland talks to Pascale Petit.

MM: I wonder if we could start by talking about your experience of writing in lockdown - has it made a difference to your process?

PP: I've hardly written anything. Usually when I've finished a book, I start on the next, but I've felt in shock. However, the writing has started to get going again. Spring will come. But not travel. Our plan to go to Nagarhole and see leopards is unlikely to happen for a while.

One of the things I have been doing is writing about Bodmin Moor, when it was forested. Part of winning the Laurel Prize was a commission to write a poem about Cornwall's AONB[1]. First it was too boggy and now it's too cold to walk there, but I'm writing about it and looking forward to taking it all in again. This is strange as I'm not writing about home. Cornwall isn't my home. Paris was, in a strange way.

MM: Many people have made Cornwall their home.

PP: I do love it here. Particularly one area which is quite deserted and not very popular. I suppose it links to the Garrigue and the Causses in South of France that I knew as a child, except those are limestone plateaux and here it's granite.

MM: Are you heading towards a book with this, or is it a wait and see?

PP: Definitely wait and see. I was commissioned to write an essay for *Granta*'s forthcoming issue on travel in the light of the pandemic. I am quite excited about it. It might end up in a collection, it's more like a very long prose poem that journeys from Paris to India... But at the moment I don't know where it will go.

MM: Is it a good place to be, not knowing?

---

1 Cornwall's Area of Outstanding Natural Beauty covers a diverse range of landscapes including Bodmin Moor, West Penwith, and the Fal, Helford and Fowey estuaries.

PP: I don't usually have a prolonged period when I'm not writing towards a book so it is exciting. I feel I'm experimenting. Using the prose form is an experiment and also the imagery – bringing the Indian forests into the cellars of Paris.

MM: That sounds intriguing. And metaphorically it's your heritage. So, in writing a first draft, what comes first: form, line, image?

PP: A number of things have to come together: an image or two, a working title – I find it really hard to write without a title. I won't have a theme to begin with. The image leads to the theme. I have to be excited by the image, or double images they often are in my poems. And the form: I'll think quickly what is this? Usually a poem. That's what's most familiar and easy, though I also have a novel that I've been working on for a long time. It's set mainly in Paris, with excerpts in South America.

MM: I remember you mentioning that when you ran your wonderful classes at Tate Modern. You'd organise games, like surreal definitions for us. Do you use prompts in your writing?

PP: I tend to image hunt, through usually contemporary art. Many poems in *Tiger Girl* and *Mama Amazonica* originated from artwork I found online.

MM: I read somewhere when you were trying to decide which discipline to follow you would do a year of each. How did the processes of sculpture and poetry compare?

PP: I found writing definitely kinder. When I was a sculptor, I did things that technically involved a lot of labour. I was always driving myself really hard. Maybe to prove myself against the male tradition; I became very proficient in using resin and fibreglass casting. I find it easier to manipulate forms and metaphors in poems than to manipulate materials in sculpture.

I don't think I could make things well enough in sculpture for the onlooker to suspend disbelief and let the magical aspects come through. Also, with poems time is more available to play with. On the other hand the material of words is also a very hard material, because words are so over-used.

MM: So, challenging, yet satisfying?

PP: What I really liked about being a visual artist, a sculptor, was being in a studio, absorbed in my own world, that world-making aspect. On the other hand, you can also make a world in a book: all neatly stored in this quite small thing... I'm always careful about my covers.

MM: You're instrumental in choosing your covers?

PP: Yes! When I moved to Bloodaxe, they said they knew this about me so would always ask me first what I'd like...

MM: Your covers are stunning. I've been enjoying rereading your books, particularly, *Tiger Girl*, and found myself wondering who your influences were. I know there's Keats, but which other poets, and how did poetry call you?

PP: I discovered Keats at school: that's how poetry discovered me. At school I was very good at a lot of subjects but only second-best in creative writing, whereas in art I was top, so felt more confident as a visual artist. I'm sure I really wanted to be a poet.

Through Keats I discovered a way of creating and of thinking organically, creating the forests and strange urn-like shapes. I suppose I expanded Keats's poems in my mind: I had sketchbooks full of Grecian urns, and was fascinated by his 'Lamia'. I've written a lot about snakes and snake women.

MM: Did you have poetry friends, a mentor?

PP: I never had a mentor and didn't have any encouragement. At art school the students I met were makers, not readers. However I was introduced to the poetry of Sylvia Plath, Ted Hughes and Peter Redgrove, and that was exciting: Hughes was this very primal force, Redgrove had incredible energy and ideas, it felt organic and sensory, and Plath was electric. I went to a few groups, but they weren't like today's workshop/ feedback groups, so it was a slow process. Especially as I was trying to write things that weren't fashionable: the taste was for city-based poetry. Then I became Poetry Editor of *Poetry London* and that taught me so much. My MA at the Royal College had disheartened me, whereas poetry was becoming more important. Eventually I became sole Poetry Editor and stayed for 15 years.

MM: I understand you were also involved in the founding of the Poetry School.

PP: That was Mimi [Khalvati]'s baby. She invited Jane Duran and myself to join her. I was one of the main tutors, though I hadn't brought out a book by then. Mimi had such faith in me.

MM: Can you remember your first published poem?

PP: That was in my 20s. I was published in *Iron:* a six-page poem about my grandmother's garden as a kind of Eden. Not unlike the poetry I'm writing now. I was also published in *The Poetry Review*, until I started writing more personal stuff, as in *The Zoo Father,* which went down less well...

MM: You say the personal is universal. What would you say to people who are afraid of being too exposing? It's as if you've found a way to put the confessional so steeped in nature that what is shocking becomes beautiful and moving.

PP: Thank you! The way I write personal poetry is to make it pleasurable. I am intensely interested in what I examine in my books: are people good, and why do they do bad things, and is there any way to redeem that? I use the material of abuse and maltreatment in my family to explore these thoughts. To make it central I write

59

through what excites me: nature at its most enthralling. This is why I would go around the world looking at wonders like Angel Falls, tigers, jaguars.

MM: Nature isn't always kind, yet in capturing the wonder and awe you make both sides understandable?

PP: Exactly. The beauty is there: tigers are beautiful, awe-inspiring. I've never actually seen a kill, but I've seen them on video and I am always scanning Instagram: there was a beautiful little fawn and this huge tiger's paw picking it up. There was something beautiful in the contrast between the helpless fawn and the tiger who is hungry. Of course, the other thing about the pandemic is that it comes from a natural source.

MM: Caused by man destroying the balance...

PP: Yes, so nature turns...

MM: Maybe it's an existential message about life and death: which brings us back to Keats, who writes of love and death both as things of beauty, a kind of romance linked to death.

PP: Yes, he said 'I have been half in love with easeful death'. He was surrounded by people dying and died pitifully young.

MM: Have you been to his grave in Rome?

PP: No, I've never been to Italy. So many countries I've not been to...

MM: At least we have books. And your poems are vivid, far from quiet or shy, although you describe yourself as shy and quiet: does this create a problem for public readings?

PP: I do find it disturbing, reading my poems. Not just for their content. I am extremely shy. As a child my reports said I was very withdrawn.

MM: Do you workshop your poems with others, in a group?

PP: I show them to my husband who is not a poet. He's a very good reader and tells me what is not alive, what works and is also good with grammar. I used to workshop, but these days I prefer the work of time.

MM: And do you write fast and edit much, or sit on them?

PP: When I'm in the writing zone I can write three or four poems a day. This is quite often how books start. I'll go back and edit them, even after they've been in magazines, and yet more editing at proof stage – that's the point when I see that first stanza is not necessary, when I see through the eyes of a reader. It depends. Some of the poems in *Tiger Girl* I hardly edited, while the last poem in *Mama Amazonica*, 'The Jaguar,' took over five weeks to get right, restarting, always recasting it.

At the moment I am working on a long poem which I started writing when I was working on *Mama Amazonica*. It didn't go in the book, but it's useful for something different I want to do. Sometimes I revive things from a notebook. Often I find a poem I thought was dead, but revisiting it three to five months later, it's not. A lot can depend on mood.

MM: And the structure of your writing day?

PP: I love writing very early in the morning, usually in bed, with a cup of tea.

MM: Do you keep a notebook by your bedside?

PP: Piles of notebooks. I stay with longhand as long as possible, but the temptation to put it on the screen is stronger than it used to be...

MM: Do you find your writing is qualitatively different longhand?

PP: Yes, because it's slower, and it has its own special feeling.

MM: And you edit less?

PP: Yes. I always enjoy writing on the page. My notebooks now have become lighter, thinner, smaller, though I like the pages to be wide, as the form is important: I want to see from the beginning what the form is.

MM: Moving on to your work as a tutor, I wonder how important mentoring is for you, what you get from it.

PP: I keep trying to give it up so I can greedily have more time for my own work, but I get a lot out of mentoring: these generally new, frequently talented poets. They keep me on my toes, teach me things!

MM: What jumps out at you with a poet you're mentoring?

PP: It varies, usually aliveness, or they have something really interesting to say, a way with words and language. I'm only mentoring these days. I've not been group tutoring online.

MM: Did that sap your energy, or were you able to write your own poems alongside?

PP: It was exciting but exhausting. I have very few poems from my nine years of Tate Modern Monday evening classes. However, I still have those artists in my mind and the monographs I bought meaning to write my own poems but never managing it...

MM: yet.

PP: It's all there. Very powerful too, like the Tornado exhibition – Francis Alÿs.

MM: Was it a good decision to move to Cornwall?

PP: Yes, it's much easier, though I miss the ease of seeing people, going to the Royal Festival Hall to do mentoring, the galleries, exhibitions. It's not the same online. But I was never really a city person.

MM: So the formative years of your upbringing were divided between Wales, Paris and the South of France?

PP: Yes, and when I was in Paris as a child I had a terrible time.

MM: You were under 10?

PP: From two and a half to seven. And a year and a half of that was spent in a children's home south of Paris. I remember being left with various neighbours, very little time spent with my mother and father... yes, a very unhappy time.

MM: And with no security, if you were just 'dumped' here and there...

PP: Absolutely. That lack of security in the first part of my life was a real hindrance because I knew I had to rely on myself to make my own security.

MM: Wales must have seemed a godsend.

PP: Yes, my grandmother was a lifesaver. I was with her from newborn to two and a half, because my mother couldn't cope, then I was taken to Paris when I was about two and a half by my aunt who was 15, and she stayed to look after us because my mother couldn't. But my aunt wasn't treated well, and eventually she escaped. There was abuse and not good memories of Paris. In my mind the countryside became good, the city bad.

MM: Then you returned to Wales when you were seven?

PP: Yes, seven till 14. We were surrounded by fields and animals... I would work in the garden for my grandmother.

MM: Growing vegetables?

PP: Everything we ate we grew and had fruit trees, and once a week or so there was the butcher's van and the sweet van...

MM: These sound like good memories.

PP: It was lovely, and I got on with my grandmother.

MM: Tiger Girl?

PP: Yes, my Indian grandmother.

MM: Did she die, was that why you returned to France?

PP: No, she died at 90. But she was getting on and we were teenagers, and she couldn't cope. My mother came to Wales for us. That's when the poetry came in because I could escape to my secret world of poems and writing.

MM: So, after 14 you spent time in the South of France?

PP: My mother had bought a vineyard in Languedoc with two stone huts and we would spend the summer holidays there with her. There were black rats and hornets in these huts, but it was wonderful.

MM: Sounds amazing... I wonder as a final thought, what advice you might offer our readers who include people who have turned to poetry later on and maybe feel disadvantaged as a result?

PP: I can only give my example - I was in my mid 40s before I published my first book. Though there was less emphasis on young new poets in those days. I would say not to be too age-obsessed, particularly where women are concerned. When I was trying to break through there were only two MA poetry courses in the whole country. These days the poetry world is very active, very sociable. My advice is to persevere, be tenacious as a bulldog.

Mary Mulholland

Books by Pascale Petit

Tiger Girl (2020)
Mama Amazonica (2017)
Fauverie (2014)
Effigies (2013)
What the Water Gave Me (2010)
The Treekeeper's Tale (2008)
The Huntress (2005)
The Wounded Deer (2005)
The Zoo Father (2001)
Heart of a Deer (1998)
Icefall Climbing (1994)

The Essay

Lesley Sharpe uncovers a 'wild patience': magic and transformation in 'Integrity' by Adrienne Rich.

The 'wild patience' that opens this poem conjures an image of something held in both a delicate balance, and an impossible tension for the speaker, a woman at a certain stage of her life. Throughout the poem we find these, and other polarities, pulling against each other, yet yoked uncomfortably tight. It is 'the quality of being complete', that epigrammatic definition of 'integrity' from Webster's Dictionary that prefaces the poem, and forms its title, that invites a resolution in a world where neither wildness nor patience is enough. 'An epigram', said Seamus Heaney, 'is like a tuning fork', and perhaps Adrienne Rich shows us that this also makes it like a spell, casting a benevolent and unifying influence which, sounding through each line of the poem, is integral to its power.

A brief glance at the etymological dictionary adds another dimension. A quixotic word of many derivations, 'spell' has evolved in one of its meanings from Old English *spala*, which came to mean *a single worker's turn at work* and finally *a period spent in a job or occupation*. Rich's poem taps into that sense of *spell* as time spent, a necessary duration which is the prerequisite of so many transformational journeys with their attendant myths, their herculean tasks, the landscapes and cycles of time that must be traversed, always without loss of vision or purpose. A wild patience, she says, 'has carried me this far'. But her subject is also motherhood, which she might be said to envision as *a single worker's turn at work, a period spent in a job or occupation,* caught always in a contradiction with the fact that, as she said, 'for me, poetry was where I lived as no one's mother, where I existed as myself.'[1]

The mythic structure of the poem plays with the resolution of seven cycles of seven years found in so many traditions. That forty-ninth year, the jubilee, embodies ideas of duration and culmination, and often it is followed by a year of rest. For the woman, retracing her way by boat to a cabin, there seem to be many things at stake on a journey 'this far north' in light 'critical', in her 'forty-ninth year', with light and time hanging in the balance. But it also contains within itself a sense of mystery, as Rich conjures:

> ...this
> long-dreamed, involuntary landing
> on the arm of an inland sea.
> The glitter of the shoal
> depleting into shadow...

---

[1] Adrienne Rich, *Of Woman Born, Motherhood as Experience and Institution* (London: Virago, 1977), p. 31.

Fulfilling a cycle, or circle, the culmination inevitably involves a return: made vividly present in colours more true, the recognized image of 'the stand of pines/violet-black really', not green as 'in the old postcard', achieves a newly concrete existence. So too does the narrative of a life lived, articulated in the long-forgotten detail of 'the chart nailed to the wallboards/the icy kettle squatting on the burner' of the cabin.

Redundant, and abandoned, the chart, as full of contradiction as that 'icy kettle', has offered no real map to navigate a life filled with frustration. For Rich the constraining force is that which is 'overlaid' on women's lives 'by societal and traditional circumstance',[2] particularly in relation to motherhood. Not 'the fact of motherhood', she writes in *Of Woman Born*, first published in 1976, two years before 'Integrity', but 'the patriarchal institution of motherhood', by which, beyond the care of children, a woman is 'restricted from acting on anything except inert materials like dust and food'.[3] Her poem revises this narrative, elevating the role of hands which have 'worked the vacuum aspirator', and 'emptied that kettle one last time'. Domestic tasks are redeemed poetically through incantation into rituals, where the anaphora of 'And I have' both bears witness to, and enlarges, the quotidian detail in stanzas which give shape to, and reshape, a whole life.

It is here we might find the poem connecting us to yet another kind of spell, those incantations of language which energise and are, finally, instrumental in that process of transformation. In her essay Rich tells us that 'as a young mother I remember feeling guilt that my explosions of anger were a bad example for my children…a defect of character, having nothing to do with what happens in the world outside one's flaming skin.'[4] But the anger of frustrated creative and intellectual impulses, which appears in the poem as a sense of being 'scalded' by the burning sun, with its association of a dominant power, also meets a contradictory tenderness, captured most powerfully in the image of hands which have 'caught the baby leaping/from between trembling legs'. Embodying both the exhilaration and exhaustion of a life demanding unconditional 'relation to others rather than the creation of self',[5] the language of 'leaping' and 'trembling' explodes with a physicality both endearing and relentless. But this physicality also yokes the speaker to the uneasy violence of 'the hand that slammed and locked' the cabin door.

Though scalded themselves, hands perform the domestic acts by which life is defined, and refined. They have 'stroked the sweated temples' of others, in repetitive movements mirrored in the alliteration and assonance of Rich's language. They have 'stopped to wreathe the rain-smashed clematis/back on the trellis', tenderly restoring it 'for no one's sake except its own'. Finally, they are even 'salved' by their own power of healing, in the discovery that, as Rich observes in another poem, 'her wounds came from the same source as her power'.[6] The 'wild

---

[2] Ibid. pp. 32–8.

[3] Adrienne Rich, *Of Woman Born, Motherhood as Experience and Institution* (Virago, 1977), pp. 32–38.

[4] Ibid. p. 46.

[5] Ibid. p. 42.

[6] 'Power', Adrienne Rich, *Adrienne Rich's Poetry and Prose (Norton Critical Editions)* (W. W. Norton & Company, 1993), p. 73.

patience' is now both fuel and spell, its 'unspoken anger' an energy compacted by time and resistance to celebrate that it is hands and words which express the rhythms of life.

That sense of spell as duration is also complete: 'I have', she says, earlier in the poem as she steers the boat in, 'nothing but myself to go by; nothing/…except what my hands can hold'. Everything else has been stripped away, leaving only 'the realm of pure necessity', and her 'selves', a settling in with the fact of this duality: 'After so long, this answer.' It is the poetic power of the spider to weave out of herself 'anywhere - even from a broken web' which provides the metaphor for the final transformation, in which the polarities of anger and tenderness can become 'angels', attendant energies[7] no longer being held in opposition to each other, suggest a transcendence which can also keep its feet firmly on the ground. It is this poetic ability to create lines 'where inner and outer reality fuse into a kind of living fabric' which, John Ashbery observed, make Rich 'a metaphysical poet'.[8] Like the spider always remaking, the poet weaves together the repetitions and contradictions, spell-like, retrieving and re-visioning: in 'Integrity', the mended 'broken web' of the spider recalls the 'unbroken condition' of Webster's definition. The task is complete, and, in a trick of language, salvation waits inside 'salve'.

Lesley Sharpe

---

[7] Rich spoke elsewhere of the attendant daimons which forced as it were, a sort of destiny or journey, energies which expressed themselves through one, and could not be ignored: '…the term demon is more useful than angel because it conveys more of a sense which involves Rich. Demon derives from the Greek *daimon*: a divine power, fate or god; in other words, some force capable of overwhelming a person – not necessarily to evil…a conflict that could result in the reshaping of the psyche along the lines of the self-attention the demon demands'. Claire Keyes, 'The Angels Chiding', in *Reading Adrienne Rich, Reviews and Revisions, 1951-81*, ed. by Jane Roberta Cooper (Michigan: The University of Michigan Press, 1984), p. 30.
[8] John Ashbery, *'Tradition and Talent'*, in *Reading Adrienne Rich, Reviews and Revisions, 1951-81*, ed. by Jane Roberta Cooper (Michigan: The University of Michigan Press, 1984), p. 217.

The Reading

Watch the video of 'Ozymandias' by Shelley
performed by LiTTLe MACHiNe

you will find Chris Hardy's Personal View on page 53

The Alchemy Spoon
YouTube Channel

https://youtu.be/tzF-MfGzL14

Reviews

Mary Mulholland reviews two intensely moving poetry books, one about child sexual abuse, the other about stillbirth. In their different ways these two poets not only give voice to the unthinkable but transform their experiences into something of harrowing beauty.

alice hiller
bird of winter
Pavilion Press, £9.99

Natalie Whittaker
Tree
Verve Poetry Press, £7.50

Alice Hiller's debut collection opens with four poems entitled 'o dog of pompeii', paralleling the devastating effects of the Vesuvius eruption and the poet's personal experience of sexual child abuse. The first line 'your howl was buried under / metres of ash and pumice' highlights the helplessness of the guard dog, chained to its studded collar, unable to escape. A young child, equally helpless, is abused at her mother's house, 'with its dark sheds' as 'a finger   moved inward'.

Excavated 'mosaics of guard dogs' at Pompeii and Herculaneum show 'this was a / protected space.' Just as a childhood home should be. The quartet of 'dog of pompeii' with the 'chained hound of my underworld' sets up the premise for the extended metaphor of the twenty-four hours of Vesuvius's eruption in AD79 as the poet revisits memories of her early sexual abuse and is ultimately able to move beyond:

> I find you at last brought back to me whole
> mosaiced to life   and risen again
>
> asking me to throw the red rubber ball
> and watch you rush towards it barking

Several poems seem to result from prompts of excavated items or mosaics, for example, 'a carbonised cradle holding a baby's bones' takes the poet to a memory of 'my amah my armour' who looked after her for her first year or so in Paris, a nurturing Amah – 'moon / of my baby night'.

The poet's early years were spent in Northern France, where poems about her father and grandmother, bonne maman, are good memories, but this was short-lived, and the moving poem 'on the shoreline', about her father's illness, illustrates how fragile life is. The first stanza of this concrete poem reflects the suddenness and force of the Vesuvius eruption, while the lines at the bottom of the page collapse onto each other like a pillar falling apart: 'papa there was no chronology for your illness'. Later in the book, in 'libation' the poet connects to him fondly through food:

68

> I love chicory in french called
>   endive   bitter cooked or raw and only harvested by torchlight
> I eat the food of the dead dressed with vinaigrette

Near the end of the book, as if the title poem has been pluralised to include the two of them, 'oiseaux d'hiver,' Hiller pays tribute to her father, who 'fledged my down into feathers' and finally 'you rise visible / at last to me papa'.

Such nurturing is in stark contrast to her mother's care, with the disjunct between 'day-mummy' and 'night-mummy': sexual abuser by night, giving her treats by day, such as:

> a ballerina from harrods
> with soft cake
> under her frosted skirt

Her mother, 'queened by her gold sheath/and ferragamo shoes', grooms her daughter as she abuses her: 'where our two bodies touch', this poem seemingly prompted by the image of a 'thracian in an unvisored helmet facing a hoplomachus in a visored helmet armed with shield and sword'. This section is followed by three powerfully symbolic pages: one blank, then two black.

The title poem comes about midway through the collection, when the 13-year-old poet is anorexic and in hospital where 'pills drop her into nothing at night and hollow out her days'. The poem seems to contain her voice together with that of her doctor:

> *you're thirteen   you must grow up* although the chaffinch keeps
>   *and separate from your mother* fluttering onto the curtain rail
>   *you can't live at home*   it is not strong enough to fly

Birds are often regarded as soul messengers, links to the other side, and there are understandably many bird references throughout the collection, suggesting this need to fly away: 'limp pheasants', 'plucked pheasants' 'double ducks', cygnet, squabs, songbird, pelican, chick, hawk and 'birds roosting /high in the ivory pines'.

Hiller's is an assured, controlled voice, adept at playing with form and syntax to maximise effect. Her writing is pared back and lyrical, giving the writing an evocative distressing beauty as she highlights childhood traumas. She includes concrete poems, found text from her own hospital records, erasure poems where word-windows on the black background are like visors in a helmet, for example, 'this happened / during winter/ inflicted devastation / disaster/'.[1] Black pages emphasise how dark this material is. Yet the tone is more of bewilderment than anger: how inexplicable it is that a human can inflict such suffering onto an innocent, that her mother was in effect Vesuvius.

Several poems carry an abject sense of aloneness: 'Elegy for an eight year old' is particularly heart-rending: she is in the classroom where there are 'fossils on

---

[1] alice hiller, *bird of winter* (Liverpool: Pavilion Press, 2021), p. 41.

the show and tell table' and soon 'the girls will be skipping in the playground', but the young poet can't move:

> mr ward says she's moving
> onto the green book for maths
>
> underneath her wool tights
> the hurt place stays on fire

Unsurprisingly winter and coldness make frequent appearances in the poems contrasting with the August heat of Vesuvius's eruption, while being a reminder that cold can also burn. From 'snowfall': 'cold says / *you are not loved'*.

In 'after a visit to the doctor' the young poet's mother 'made me leave the house with no top on', then, in 'december 1976' Hiller remembers, 'on christmas eve we set /angels above candles' and she passes 'warmed mince pies' to her mother's 'smart friends' knowing:

> when all the frost has melted
> my worshipped body will be as heavy
> as the grey sky above st katherine's
> where we will kneel side by side
> while the vicar says *our father*

Later in the book, when she is released from hospital, another voice starts to make itself heard, perhaps the poet's higher self, the imagined voice of her father, or a doctor: in 'let none of this enter you' the young poet is urged 'do not pee in your pants /to smell like your mother'. In 'uprising in blue and silver' the poet's 'anger rings the anvil', and there is a sense of a new order coming in.

In 'Vesuvius', she wants to 'scour out our hurt let grief melt the ash' to allow redemption and transformation, which are always possible, and sometimes we need to go beyond immediate family to find our tribe. The poet finds teenage love, 'imprint of a young woman' which is 'to become a key / in the lock of the world', and a lightness, a joy creeps in. In 'sea level' she writes: although 'there will always be the city / beneath this city', it is possible to 'swim free'.

In 'mothered' there is a suggestion of gynaecological illness overcome and the need to mother oneself: 'I live'. The collection ends with a poem to the goddess Isis, where, moving from Roman to Egyptian mythology, the poet dedicates herself to the goddess-role-model for women, particularly regarding healing and in rites for the dead, offering 'my voice / until this ibis fly / free of the carvings'.

This collection bears witness to the resilience of human nature, with poetry giving voice to the silences within that are so hard to talk about. Yet they must be voiced, and Alice Hiller has turned her devastating childhood experiences into a narrative of transformation that everyone should read.

Natalie Whittaker's experience is also unimaginably distressing, yet the honesty and simplicity with which she communicates grief and sadness cannot fail to touch any reader: these are poignant poems and testimony to Whittaker's strength as a poet. They speak equally about the fragility of time and life.

This is Whittaker's second pamphlet, and her language is now more pared back, sparing in its use of capitals, unpunctuated, giving a sense of there being no beginning or end.

In the opening poem, which is also the title poem, 'tree', the reader can imagine a mother-to-be seeing familiar things and projecting a future: 'look baby autumn / next year I'll show you autumn   and it will be so beautiful'. Then she throws in 'it's November / bare branches have faulty umbilical cords' and the poet is plunged into the month of the dead. A well-meaning 'Deren calls us all hun' but this is a support group of 'broken moth women'. She recalls the first week, with the 'small black flies'. Like thoughts you can't be rid of.

I found the 'departures' sequence particularly moving. In the first the poet's skilful use of and shifts in repetition, 'we leave the hospital   without out baby' culminate in the powerful ending 'we've left our love   our baby   in / a morgue   the night is lowered'. The second part is equally affecting by way of the gaps and the pared back language:

> we leave the funeral   without her ashes
> we're told there wouldn't be enough of her
> to hold on to

The third part remembers a life before: 'when we were young/ we thought departures   meant leaving on a train'. 'insomnia' seems to be about the passing of time, eight moons are mentioned. There is a sense of trying to recover some structure to life. In 'teaching GCSE English', though Whittaker includes quotes from Macbeth, Romeo and Juliet, and reference to Gillian Clarke and Priestly, 'there are landmines / waiting under fields   I   once   owned'. Grieving has its own timescale.

The poet turns to images from the seashore: in 'little hermit crab' the poet writes, 'your tiny hand curled / on the beach of me', and in 'tides' she stands 'on a black beach / hacked   by white water'. Then in 'clocks' acknowledging the way grief makes its own time, the poet writes: 'I'm sure yesterday was June' but finds it's one year on and 'a bomb has gone off inside me'. In her 'google search history' she questions 'how long to grieve a baby' returning once more to 'tree' where she is now the object of interest to a consultant and medical students discussing 'our rare and bitter fruit'. But, finally, 'spring' comes, and 'a beat says *mum / live   live   live'*.

The book is dedicated to Whittaker's stillborn daughter and is a hauntingly beautiful study of the poet's experience of stillbirth, but far more than that.

Mary Mulholland

Diana Cant looks at two collections that, in their very different ways, throw light into the spaces of body and mind.

Katie Griffiths
The Attitudes
Nine Arches Press, £9.99

Tiffany Atkinson
Lumen
Bloodaxe, £10.99

Katie Griffiths grew up in Canada, in a family originally from Northern Ireland. In 2019 she was awarded second place in the National Poetry Competition for her poem 'Do not indulge indigo', and her pamphlet *My Shrink is Pregnant* was published by Live Canon Press. This is her debut collection.

It seems important to start with some unambiguous facts because Griffith's dazzling and dancing collection has a slippery, shape-shifting quality – as soon as the reader feels themselves to be on solid ground, they are drawn down a trail of associations and wordplay that can lead to some very unexpected places.

The title of the collection is a reference to The Beatitudes, the eight blessings delivered by Jesus during the Sermon on the Mount. In Griffith's hands, religion, and especially Catholic imagery and sonority, weave throughout these poems, often in ironic and witty ways:

> Insipid are the moonbathers
> for their light spills in small places
>
> Torrid are those who amass
> for their trinkets will devour

and, as you become accustomed to the often playful poetic voice, you notice that the initial word of each 'blessing' ends in 'id' – surely no coincidence. The poet invites the reader to join her in a game of associative 'hide and seek', which belies a more serious purpose, for these are poems that examine questions of faith, death, and how to occupy a space on earth. Threading throughout is a series of poems entitled 'Dough must not enter the body' – immediately referencing eating disorders, but with a profound seriousness:

> …trying to occupy
>
> less space yet at the same time
> disturb it more. For wasn't that
>
> the communion wafer's trick
> on the tongues of the pious?
>
> To dissolve. Disappear.
> Do the holy work.

A sharp intelligence and fizzing wit counterbalance the serious, a wit that is both playful and teasing. It is this teasing quality that can upend the reader. For example, 'Nine sort-of-truths' has a series of three annotations at the end, each leading us further from the poem by playing with truth and containing the fabricated (?) quote 'no matter if the reader is irretrievably lost between lines, missing, presumed dead.'

Lines from one poem may lead directly to another on the opposite page, as in 'My best canvas', where the line 'I've nailed it / as you would a winding cloth' prefigures 'I'll be the nail on the Wittenberg door' in 'Up Yours, Wittenberg!' Or, the poem 'The winter inside my mother', which sits opposite the poem 'snow is mutiny', in which the faint-print text (symbolising snow?) surrounds the darker prose print, as if a burial chamber or womb. And the title of that poem is repeated at the end of another. Thus, the reader is invited to follow a series of seductive clues and associations, which can range from Cat Stevens, Rapunzel, Gilbert and Sullivan and the Bible. Ancient sings inventively with modern throughout, as in 'Earthmonger' – 'Let them fashion from your rib a comely robot.'

In the midst of this cleverness and creativity, there are often beautifully lyrical lines:

'I sieve daylight / across a piece of paper'
'snow that has the smell of linger'
'what is fecundity / if not loud and overbearing'

And, from 'Biography':

She spreads across him as ivy across a wall.
If she thieves light
it is only because of his complicit mortar.

Griffiths has a fondness for a turn, or, more frequently, a vertiginous plunge at the end of a poem that often leaves the reader with the shock of mortality. In 'And in our idleness we compare hands', a poem seeming to deal with exorcism, and the first of the collection, we are suddenly faced with the last lines:

I say, I held my father close
those last minutes before his hands
dropped like starfish
learning the ocean.

This 'dying fall' happens often and is an important counterpoint to some of the tricky 'diagonal moves' which 'enjoy the skulduggery' that Griffiths can employ. She highlights the interface between sharp intelligence, and a more profound, emotional way of being in the world. Often, rather than emotional intimacy with another, the place of 'the other' is occupied by the untrustworthy legacy and language of religion.

These are complex, rich and restless poems. Those who like their poetry to convey a sense of emotional 'settledness' and resolution may be disappointed here.

Griffiths will not settle for easy answers – these are poems in which matters remain un(re)solved, and are much the more powerful for it.

***

Tiffany Atkinson is a poet and Professor of Poetry at UEA. This, her fourth collection, illustrates her continuing preoccupation with the body and its conjunction with emotional life. Her writing is often wry and ironic without being sardonic. Consequently, many of the poems vibrate with a capacity for compassion, coupled with an ability to stand back and make detached, intelligent observation. This can result in edgy, discomforting writing.

The opening sequence, 'Dolorimeter', is a disquisition on the nature of pain, written as a result of a residency at Bronglais Hospital in Wales. A dolorimeter is a hypothetical device for measuring pain, and these poems are a moving assembly of different attempts to describe pain, and the way it slips away from being pinned to language. Some are 'found' poems, originating from notices on hospital walls, or from the overheard scraps of the conversations of patients. Atkinson says she was 'just listening to people tell me stories', but that belies the delicate skill needed to gather these scraps into a whole that embodies tenderness as well as terror. For example, from 'Socrates', written in response to a pain check-list:

> Site – *Where is the pain?*
>   In the violet corners
>   Under my tongue
>   at the root of language
>   At the bottom of my red bag   ringing all hours
>   Jesus how can you ask that
> > > > *Here   Here   Here*

Atkinson excels at catching the ordinary traces of life and adding the unexpected, as in the office-girls leaving Lemsip on the desk of a consultant with a cold as they adjust 'the magnolias of paper-work', or, after a tea-break, seeing 'a minor coin / of new shit in the loo's bleached font'.

Pain's relationship to language is also explored – on the one hand pain is a vital sign, 'Look for the one / who's drawn himself in / like a stone', but on the other:

> We are trying to avoid the word *pain*
> It is far too full of itself   This
>
> is less a problem of language
> than a problem of belief

Threading through this sequence, and indeed the whole collection, is a sense of the duality of things: what is inside or outside, up or down, transcendental or ordinary. The second part of the collection begins with the long prose poem, 'You can't go there'. Here is Atkinson at her most witty, while also addressing the painful landscape of infertility and IVF, in a parallel 'narrative' about her beloved 'red dog', and by the contrast between mourning and melancholia (using both Freud's paper 'Mourning and Melancholia', and Lars von Triers' film *Melancholia*). This manages to be both affecting and witty, with an ironic personal register that carries us with her. Her descriptions of the dog's unabashed joy – 'consider how he tackles his marrow-bone balancing it between his gold wrists like an ice-cream cone and pushing his tongue into the sweet hole' – contrasts with the murkier terrain of melancholia, IVF and the unresolved grieving for a child that never was: 'Cruel optimism is another word for *trying* IVF has much in common with the slippery syntaxes of meritocracy'. We are again in the province of 'inner work' in several senses.

The remainder of this collection looks at the world of work, and the insider/outsider dilemma. 'Panels' and 'The department of small arts' take a slant view of academia, and the witty 'Workshop', reminiscent of the Billy Collins poem of the same name, depicts the familiar struggle of workshopping poetry. 'It is a very gracious hotel' has a wonderful rhythm and sonority – an almost incantatory feel towards the end – which repays reading out loud, as indeed do many of the poems.

> I have been the man and I have been the woman I have been
> the night receptionist revising by the phone I've been the manager
> descending from his ante-room like Moses

And more dog poems: Atkinson is a self-confessed dog-lover and owner and the dog can come to represent many things, frequently symbolising the contrast between spontaneous joy and self-conscious introspection, public and private, inner and outer.

> Red dog shitting
> plants his four stars in the grass
> and up goes the tent of himself
> his tail pegged out
> his eyelids fine and private, And I think
>   so that's how we do all things with the body.

Atkinson's poems are intent on tackling 'the quandary of what's inside', and doing so with a cool, intelligent beauty, offset by wit and serious personal reflection. The cover of this book is a thing of beauty in itself.

Diana Cant

Sara Levy looks at a pamphlet and a collection which have in common only that they are both honest and unflinching in their gaze.

Luke Wright
The Feel-Good Movie Of The Year
Penned in the Margins, £9.99

Chaucer Cameron
In An Ideal World I'd Not Be Murdered
Against the Grain Press, £6.00

This, Luke Wright's third collection, employs a more confessional style in his poems than his previous writing to explore personal themes of love, loss and longing. In doing so he delves into striking the balance between the often-conflicting roles of father, friend, son, performer, party animal, lover. The collision of these themes is addressed in 'The Rack', with Wright acknowledging, 'I am both: a single parent on the Brexit coast and / dumbstruck lover on Brighton's shingle shore'.

The collection is bookended by 'Ex', and 'The Turning on the Halesworth Road', both written about a marriage breakup, in controlled, measured language from the position of someone who has calmly stepped back to let the dust settle:

> not even an x at the end
> of a text. I'm not saying
>
> that I want to. I just wonder
> where we went...

In between, the reader travels alongside the poet, through the highs and lows of friendships lost and found, new love, fatherhood and wistfully recalled childhood memories which take on poignant significance when the reader understands the responsibility of being a parent. This is captured tenderly in the refrain 'to keep an eye on you' in 'Prayer', and the family outings to his father's London office in, 'To Hail a Cab', when 'he'd step out of the lift, pinstriped / and powerful, somehow taller than at home.'

There is a melancholy sense of time ticking away in many of the poems, perhaps instilled in the poet by his father, whose hobby of constructing timepieces is fondly recalled in 'Clocks'. The reader feels the heart-warming sense of fatherly pride that pervades this collection:

> You crept into my room
> to uncase the gold medal
>
> you had won and whispered
> *Pretty good eh?*
> You let me in...

In 'Reading for Pleasure', Wright captures the magic of a moment of transformation in childhood when the door to self-led reading opens and:

> Seconds, minutes, whole hours slip by
> Now words can hold you, steady
> as a rock pool. The power of this…

It is in these poems about the experiences of parenthood that the reader encounters the raw swell of love. In 'Merch Stall', dad and son working together:

> I sign the books and you collect
> the cash. You're eight, as careful with money
> as you are with love…

In 'A Pub Gig In The Middle Of Nowhere' Wright gives the reader a devastating acknowledgement of the limits on precious family time:

> …which I, through work
> and through divorce, have cleaved
>
> in two. Have taken half of.
> Dear God. Only half.

Wright's writing is both sharp and searing, panning in and out from past to present, from the euphoria of 'Clouds' where 'I'm dissolving like an aspirin in the clear lake of the sky', to the soul-baring desperation of 'Akrasia', to the pastoral idyll of the River Waveney on the Suffolk/Norfolk border with its 'streamer weed and pennywort' in 'And I Saw England'.

Fans of Wright's more journalistic style and exuberant spoken-word performances will not be disappointed. There is the familiar fizz and fire of social outrage, and his irreverent humour rings out in 'We're Back at the End Again', and shakes the bars of the cage in 'Monster' and 'Bring Me My Devil':

> God I miss my devil! Shitting like a
> barn owl down my back, whispering his
> slanders in my ear…

These breathless, powerful poems are brilliantly contrasted with moments of quiet contemplation when the reader is diverted away from the path to encounter something calmer and more introspective. One wonders if the castle motif in 'Portcullis' and 'Drawbridge' might be Wright's safe retreat:

> I suppose it's time to tidy up.
> Raise the drawbridge, fill the moat
> and gather wood for winter…

There is a sense of vulnerability in the opening line 'My poor old heart, I left its drawbridge down / all summer long, encouraged in the strangers.' Is it a sense of over-exposure on the page that makes the poet ask 'What adult / holds a party in their heart / and broadcasts the address?'

This collection is well-crafted and full of surprises embodying stark contrasts of mood and shade, and exploring what it takes to become a man, and to survive. The poet invites his reader to join him as he navigates a path on the journey to achieve that elusive sense of equilibrium, acknowledging that 'it's all in the feel, like locating a vein, knowing when / to drop the bass, or finding the biting point'.

***

Chaucer Cameron's debut pamphlet is a startling and challenging piece of work, simultaneously bold, bleak and beautifully written. It gives an account of a life many readers will not recognise or relate to. Part memoir, part fiction, it documents the lived experiences of sex workers in a voice which is both honest and controlled. The reader is invited to witness through Cameron's eyes the day-to-day reality of prostitution, and the grim underbelly of violence, exploitation and risk that it inhabits.

The opening poem, '128 Farleigh Road', establishes the poet's unflinching hold over her reader in the lines 'But here we are, just he and I gazing at each other / the way dead people do when caught together intimately'.

The sequence of four short, devastating poems which comprise 'Body Marks' are laid out sparsely on the page, making powerful use of the white space to slow down the reader and allow them to fully process each story, each named woman, as here, in 'Inside Forearm':

> *I am a palimpsest,* she said,
> *beneath this rose tattoo – a barcode –*
>   *(Morgan)*

Several of the poems consider the physical and emotional self-preservation these women use to cope and survive, from switchblades to substances. In 'King's Cross Café (I)' the poet reflects on the coping mechanism of stepping out, talking about oneself in the third rather than the first person to create a distance:

> Crystal would always talk about her body
>   *A body bought and sold ages so much faster*
> as if it wasn't real – wounds – scars –

or the act of emotional removal, stepping outside of the escalating danger to retreat back to a safer time, as in 'Cartoons':

> It's funny what you think of when you're gagging/ for your life
> when you hear the car doors/ click/
> when the music is turned up/ and you put on your disguise.
> Tonight/ it was the Flintstones/ I watched them as a kid/...

There is no sugar-coating and many of the poems are harrowing in their frank portrayal of sex work, the minimalist language intensifying the dehumanization and commodification of women and young girls. In 'Trixie is A Whore' we read:

> She says she's sixteen, but I don't believe her.
> She's tiny, still tight…
>
> Rate her – 8/10

It is a tribute to the poet's artistry that she delicately negotiates a fine line, balancing the graphic with the mundane, 'A miscarriage, abortion, I can't remember which…the foetus ended up in the dustbin…Just a cramp or two, a bleed, a full stop'.

Dark truths sit side by side with flashes of humour as in 'Administration' where the reader is introduced to Amy who:

> …worked in admin,
> met clients in the office.
> Evenings it was shorthand.
>
> *Oh hello, Mr Carter.*
> *Yes, I've nearly finished.*
> *It's so nice of you to come, and so quickly.*

Even in the bleakest of moments, there is no sense of judgment or victimhood. Cameron artfully reminds the reader these are real women, their names keep appearing in parentheses beneath the poems, reinforcing their reality as multi-faceted individuals who happen to do this job, keeping begonias, decorating their bedsits with art posters, just wanting to live somewhere quiet '*but not so quiet I get murdered'*.

The language of the poet is calm and controlled, even when describing knife-edge precariousness, as she gives voice to an often-unvoiced sector of society. At the end of the book, Cameron acknowledges the help and support she received from various sources in 'saying the difficult thing'. It can have been no easy task, but it has been done skilfully. These poems challenged and stayed with me. I felt moved and enriched by Cameron's writing, and was left with a strong sense of survival and positivity with which many of these poems are imbued.

The launch of this pamphlet in March coincided with International Sex Workers' Rights Day and is a valuable addition to the conversation regarding societal attitudes to sex work and how, as a society, we can strive to keep sex workers safe.

Sara Levy

Vanessa Lampert reviews Dom Bury's first collection, ten years in its making, which maintains a steady, almost obsessively penetrating gaze in order to examine themes of environmental degradation and collapse, and asks, from such ashes, what might be saved?

Dom Bury
Rite of Passage
Bloodaxe, £10.99

Bury announces the themes of his book at its outset, simultaneously brilliantly raising the status of his poetry by dividing the book into the four sections: KYRIE, DIES IRAE, LIBERA ME and IN PARADISM.

In this framing of his work in the Latin of the Christian liturgy, Bury gestures towards and sensitively honours ideas of the divine which weave through and bind his collection. This is less a book to dip into, than one to first read from cover to cover and sit with the pain of it for a while.

In 'The Chapel in the Sea', the poem's speaker is both human and Christ-like, with 'residues of old wounds' where birds shuffle 'like pilgrims   to place offerings / at my feet. Later in the same poem, 'a dove / with its burnt wings   spread out / nailed fast into the cross' announces the creatures of the animal kingdom which suffered and suffer still, appearing as metaphors for the crucified Christ.

These poems insist that the meaning and impact of the way humans choose to live must be considered within the contexts of both spiritual understanding and humanity's behavioural impact upon the natural world. The imagery in these poems frequently juxtaposes what is humanly created and what is beyond human control to powerful and memorable effect. In 'Snow Country', 'Lightning opens the sky / like a flung knife' asserting the truth of humankind's violent actions against the natural world and their consequences for it.

As word art, a poem announces its status by being framed upon the page. Bury skilfully extends this trope by creating, within his poetry, windows between the natural, divine and human worlds, reminiscent of religious iconography offering windows to humankind's notions of a heavenly kingdom. These poems often reference and name 'God'. 'Passageway' describes the bird that 'scratches its talons / against the will of God / not knowing / that sometimes / the darkest passageway / is the only true way to emerge / out into the light.'

While Bury persistently positions his reader in the dark passageways of humankind's own making, the appearances of his poems are in the main passages of text extravagantly spaced and broken up by white space. This is reminiscent of how nature returns in abundance to fill the spaces winter creates. How apposite it is that this book should be published in springtime.

So consistent is the sense of airy spaciousness in Bury's work, that where his poetry lets in less light, its reader turning the page to encounter a boulder of words, a roadblock in the flow, this serves to catch the reader's attention, thereby cleverly augmenting its message. In 'Afterwards' Bury offers the idea of hope. The opening words of the poem are offered to the reader as a companion to its speaker: 'It is in fact remarkably hard to kill / something completely'. A few lines further down, the speaker invites the reader to a greater intimacy: 'Let us build something more / than what we believe our bodies are capable of – / if what we believe is human is broken.'

These poems unflinchingly maintain their focus upon themes of human-made environmental disaster, yet are never moralising. Rather they seem to be given to us by a poet who asks his reader to kneel down beside him as his equal. By opening the collection in the language of prayer, Bury foregrounds for its duration what is lost and cannot be found. 'Hiraeth' asserts the irreversible nature of the destruction humankind has wreaked upon its planet. 'And though it moves in me still – the sea, I know I can't return / to that same shore the tide, that time has now dragged closed'.

This poetry is fierce and tender. Its creator masterfully merges these two qualities. The title of 'Our Species' is accusatory, blunt in the light of its subject, yet it is lyrical, beautiful in six lines, wrought with brevity.

> Two rooks in a white field –
> one sings, sings the morning in,
> the other
>   three days without food
> kills
> the first bird's children.

Here, insomuch as it is possible to condense the central message of a book as mighty as this, lies the truth of nature's savagery: its inherent drive to live.

'Rite of Passage' has as its title the idea of change from one state of being to another, as described in Bury's National Poetry Competition winning sestina 'The Opened Field' in which the poet imagines rituals for the boys in his poem to partake in and endure so as to demonstrate their masculinity.

This is a book which embeds humankind in the natural world which exists far beneath the sky. It is a book that leaves its reader with hope, should we humans choose to be humbled enough to undertake the greatest rite of passage of all, to change.

> [...] the wheeling buzzard calls.
>
> It says
> listen, to what I ask of you –
> stand out tonight
>
> under the dark sky, wait
> for a greater pulse
> to rise up through you there.
>
> Let it guide you
> towards resurrection.

Vanessa Lampert

Sue Wallace-Shaddad reviews two very different collections which both bring history to life. We are taken to the poverty of the East End, London, in the 1870s in Judith Willson's *Fleet* and to the scourge of AIDS in the 1980s in Sue Burge's *Confetti Dancers*.

Judith Willson
Fleet
Carcanet, £11.99

Sue Burge
Confetti Dancers
Live Canon, £9.99

The cover of Judith Willson's collection, 'Fleet', has a river-like design with elements of erasure. This seems very apt for poems about history and the passage of time. Willson uses a range of poetic styles and themes to build a narrative about the historical figure, Eliza, including metaphorical themes of cages, birds and rivers.

The collection is bookended by a brief article from the *East London Observer* dated June 15, 1878, which reports that 'Eliza S —— was charged with deserting her infant children and that she was sentenced to 'three months' with hard labour'. The first part of the collection paints a picture of the East End. In 'The London Cage', we are shown typical life: 'early morning, a sudden smell of bread. A boy / running barefoot without a sound'.

'A map of roads and navigable waters' describes a young man who has come to the city. He is someone who has 'three dates of birth'. The implicit references to migration could equally be about today. 'West India Dock' incorporates found text from a wall plaque adding to the sense of historical place: '*a Provident Legislature*'. Contemporaneous quotations add colour: '*O barley-sugar temples*'. The history of the sugar trade, based on slavery, suffuses the words at the centre of the poem:

> rums   mahoganies   dye woods
> sugar warehouses   crystallising sugar*   its lustre
>
> > *free-grown in casks
> > slave-grown in boxes   distinct

The East End teems with Dickensian life. Eliza is imagined as a 'Bird-dealer's wife'. She is also described as a 'widow bird' and as 'Ask-no-questions Eliza' in 'Eliza in the laundry'. A sentence, '*She said she did not desert the children.*', taken from the newspaper article, is included in this poem. The word 'said' is also emphasised in 'I press my eye to a paper peepshow', where we are told '*Mr John Barnes said. / The magistrate said.*', then later '*She said. / The prisoner said.*' Eliza is not given the courtesy of her name. The word acts as a drumbeat like a gavel hitting the desk during sentencing. In 'The prisoner said', the title phrase is repeated three times. There is a poignancy and finality in the lines:

the only words she spoke in her life
that anyone recorded,
pressed into lead.

Four poems entitled 'Children's Song' thread through the first half of the collection, acting like a refrain. The reader may well be touched by the child's voice in the first 'Song': *'and he left us there together / like the seashells in his shop'*. The second 'Song' describes how the children's father placed stones and thistles in the cages but the reader also learns:

> *we held very still*
> *in the white stones and thistles*
> *of our father's tongue*

In the third 'Song', the father *'was brass / and his words a locked cage'* whereas the mother (Eliza) *'was water / and light on water'*. The fourth 'Song' has echoes of the nursery rhyme 'Ten Green Bottles'. The children have become birds that fly away one by one.

The prose section, 'Haunting Eliza', marks the beginning of a shift in our attention from the City of London to farther East: marshland and the Essex coast. The narrator is very present as she visits East London Cemetery to try to find where Eliza was buried. She writes 'Eliza was within touching distance of my life'[1] but comes to the conclusion 'Everything about this story is unknowable'.[2]

The final section, 'In the marsh country', opens with a poem, *'Map'*, written in three widely spaced columns. This fragmented form implies wide-open skies and land; the white space lets in *'altered light'*. *'Old Hall Marshes'* uses double-spaced lines to bring emptiness into the poem where a figure appears and disappears, perhaps an 'After image' as mentioned in the prose section.[3] The present-day bumps into history in 'Rotherhithe' with the description of finding objects on the shoreline: 'freckled earthenware' and 'Chunk of fogged glass'. There is a sense of erosion throughout the poem expressed in 'the river has ground away their exactness' and Willson indents text reflecting the scattered deposits left by the river. She writes 'I have dropped into river time'.

'About time' comprises a sequence of three very different meditations on time. The first poem links us back to the search for Eliza in the cemetery, but the poet also considers 'An after-image I cannot blink away: […] My own shade / lying down under the trees'. In the second poem, Willson plays on the word 'catch' ending with the line 'catch the light / catch the light in its fall'. The last poem beautifully invokes water, mist and mud and we feel the ghost of Eliza haunting this landscape:

> folded in shadows   mist over mirror-water
> breath on a mirror   when she died
> she left nothing   not even her death

---

[1] Judith Willson, *Fleet* (Manchester: Carcanet, 2021), p. 35.
[2] Ibid p. 40.
[3] Ibid p. 39.

In Willson's final poem, 'Corset shop window in the East End', she enjoins us to 'Think of Eliza, think her / glancing shadow'.

This atmospheric collection shows how history can be brought to life. One individual, though forgotten in time, is remembered through Willson's thoughtful poetry and prose.

***

Sue Burge takes us to many places, both actual and metaphorical in *Confetti Dancers*. The collection starts with poems based in Russia and Eastern Europe, before moving into dance-themed poems about the AIDS epidemic, also Russia-related, then a range of family poems, often about her mother. The final poems include ekphrastic poems about war and poems relating to the current pandemic. The title of the book comes from the poem 'Confetti Dancers' which compares dancers to confetti – this is an image both light and transient which is suggestive of life: we live on borrowed time.

The collection is rich in references, whether to Russian poets Alexander Ulanov, Irina Mashinski. Maria Stepanova, the Israeli poet Yehuda Amichai, the Russian filmmaker Tarkovsky, or dancers like Nijinsky and Nureyev. 'The Distractor Brides of St Petersburg' captures the tradition of Russian brides being photographed against city landmarks. The passers-by (about to be pickpocketed) are 'uninvited witnesses of breathless promises / hanging in the air like frozen banners.' The pull of Russia is outlined in 'Mother Russia': 'she dances shadowy visions / of home across her whiteness' for the dancers who are 'deciphering the beguiling codes / of western winds'.

There are effective references to film in several poems. In 'Edit', Burge builds up a detailed scene of different characters in the street who are 'walk-off parts in a film', and later writes:

> the dead are no longer in frame
> aftermath makes us all squeamish

> so scatter their parts on the cutting room floor

Tarkovsky's science fiction film, *Stalker,* is featured in the poem 'Triangulation'. This poem in three parts has a fragmented form like snippets on the cutting floor. 'Come, come my little witch' and Maria Stepanova's adaptation of 'hush a bye baby' (trans. Sasha Dugdale) anticipate the next poem 'Scapegoat' which conjures up dark fairy tales with the repetition of 'A witch walks in a forest':

> This is where rumours are birthed
> and rise like woodsmoke
> whispering of plague difference fear.

The heart of the collection comprises poems about people close to the poet, such as her dancer friend Bryce (featured in a dedication poem), who died of AIDS. An acute sense of hurt comes across in 'Royal Academy of Dancing 1981', whether the pain of a dancer's 'blistered, bleeding feet' or the suffering linked to AIDS: 'The disease is here but we don't know it, no-one's missing yet.' 'Last Supper' is a poignant evocation of a group of friends ending: 'I only remember what we didn't talk about, / that silent assassin that took you all.'

The poet also does not flinch from writing about the pain of living through her mother's illness and death. In 'Restoration', Burge depicts finding one of her mother's pills and encapsulates the stress of the situation in 'The front door is still open wide / to let the sunshine in, the drama out.' 'Mother, folded small', one of the ten prose poems in the collection, deals with darker moments of illness: 'On those days the pill bottles would be in a different order. Emptier.' In 'Laundry Marks' we read of:

> her failing eyes, fingers bent like commas,
> her toes fighting downwards, downwards
>
> towards the certain knowledge of cul-de-sac.

Burge pauses before shifting focus to these family poems in the second half, with an 'Interlude' in the form of a long poem 'Read Their Lips' *(responses to the 1916 documentary film "Battle of the Somme"* [...]). The initial section uses an anaphora, 'how', very effectively: 'How they pluck at the past, / how it runs through their fingers'. We are then sharply moved into close-up by the word 'Cut'. The poem turns into a series of frames. It uses film vocabulary, panning back and forth with sections separated out by the word 'cut'. The poem ends with the powerful image of men 'ghosting the sky like a new constellation / whispering *inconnu inconnu inconnu'*.

The collection is full of visual imagery. In the poem 'Zone', 'December closes, like a coffin lid, / over the unnourished land;' and 'the moon rises, a brief howl of light,'. In the powerful poem, 'Dreamwalking', we read of 'bruises on my arm – / five perfect purple screams'. 'Cento' draws on Alexander Ulanov's lyrical images, creating new lines from his words: 'Florist, your bones are made of untouched night / lime is in your dreams, snow in your hands'.

There is a great love of language throughout. Ballet terms are frequently incorporated, adding their own special music. In 'Confetti Dancers', the boys' dance moves are portrayed: 'jeté, fouetté, cabriole'. The found poem, 'Positions', uses the different foot positions to explore AIDS, *'a virus with no morality //'*. 'Taboo' plays on the word AIDS; its four letters are 'The smallest container for such enormity / like cupped hands with the world pouring through'.

The last three poems take the reader into the current 'war' against the coronavirus. 'Glow' ends the collection on a hopeful note: 'the generosity of the bright night sky will show us how to navigate this fearful newness'.

This collection ranges over a wide range of experience with real strength and depth. Burge reminds us of battles fought which risk being forgotten as the world moves on to deal with the next challenge.

Sue Wallace-Shaddad

Roger Bloor reviews a comprehensive collection of essays probing and analysing contemporary poetry by a Nobel Prize winning poet.

Louise Glück
American originality - essays on poetry
Carcanet, £14.99

This first UK edition of the collection of essays by 2020 Nobel Laureate Louise Glück contains an examination of the nature of American society, a society she describes as 'famously, a nation of escaped convicts, younger sons, persecuted minorities, and opportunists', which she uses as an allegory of the poetic craft.

These chapters are complemented by a series of essays exploring the writing of ten poets whose work she has reviewed or judged, and the collection ends with a series of more personal essays concerning the development of her poetic sense.

Glück's focus in the first section of the book is on the tensions, both in American society and in literature, between originality, the 'breaking of new trails' and the creation and appreciation of the value of tradition. She sees tradition as being derived from originality which is able to function 'as a model or template, binding the future into coherence and, simultaneously, though less crucially, affirming the coherence of the outstripped past.'.

Originality which does not afford the possibility of replication or continuation she describes as 'a dead end'. In an expansive and encompassing chapter titled 'American Narcissism', Glück traverses the poetry of Whitman, Dickinson, Rilke, Williams and others to develop an argument that much contemporary poetry arises from a sense that 'the self is of limitless interest'. Such literature she states follows a formulaic and often incoherent pattern which lacks meaning or direction and has the same half-life as a Japanese meal, disappearing and evaporating shortly after being consumed.

> ...formulaic because all world event directly sponsors a net of associations and memories, in which the poet's learning and humanity are offered up like prize essays in grade school; and incoherent because, though the poems go on at great length, the overall impression is that there is no plausible self generating them.

Her criticism of some modern poetry is clearly stated, her distrust of what she views as dead end narcissism, forms of poetry that have become 'not an extension of the self but a substitute for the self'.

Glück's analysis of contemporary poetry continues in her chapter 'Ersatz Thought' where she focuses on forms of 'incompleteness' in poetry, 'the repetition, accumulation, invocation of the void through ellipsis, dash, etc.'. She describes these as being used by some writers as 'tricks' and compares them to swimmers competing to see who can hold their breath under water for longest, which she feels makes 'dull watching'. Her concerns with regard to both these voids and the use of non sequitur as a style is that they can become overused and derivative and abandon the innovation and freshness of the technique in favour of the overthought, the prefabricated and predictable.

Glück is not dismissing these techniques as facile or without a place but rather questioning the judgment of poets as to how effective they are: 'The gesture, the protest, aren't in themselves dangerous. Merely: their fertility has been miscalculated.' Indeed in essays previously published she has affirmed her love of such techniques: 'I am attracted to ellipsis, to the unsaid, to suggestion, to eloquent, deliberate silence. The unsaid, for me, exerts great power: often I wish an entire poem could be made in this vocabulary.'[1]

She continues in two further essays to dissect out the detail of a series of poems, comparing and contrasting reality and fantasy, lyric and narrative with comparative discussions of Pinsky and Dobyns:

> ...where Pinsky is essentially meditative, the poems elaborating themselves in coils and spirals, Dobyns's poems are a rapid downward trajectory, the poems' accumulating mass increasing their speed. Where Pinsky is speculative, Dobyns is apocalyptic,...

This forensic and illuminating analysis of poetic style continues with reprints of her introductions of 10 poets whose work she has judged for a variety of prizes over the years. Each of these short essays is in itself a mini seminar on style and craft. Her praise and comment on each poet, whilst fulsome, is tempered by her wider view of the nature of contemporary poetry. She never hesitates to reinforce her position with regard to the importance of 'authenticity and unnerved originality' and the avoidance of studied artifice:

> 'We live in a period of great polarities: in art, in public policy, in morality. In poetry, art seems, at one extreme, rhymed good manners, and at the other, chaos. The great task has been to infuse clarity with the passionate ferment of the inchoate, the chaotic.'

The final section of the book moves to a more introspective exploration of poetic style. Using examples from her early life, and the time she spent undergoing psychoanalysis, Glück develops these essays as a platform to explore her experiences in detail and relate them to her development both as a poet and a critic. In this collection of sharply focussed and insightful essays one unifying theme emerges. Despite all the fads and fashions, the dead ends and new waves of poetry one thing survives, and that as she so vividly reminds us, is poetry: 'Poetry survives because it haunts and it haunts because it is simultaneously utterly clear and deeply mysterious; because it cannot be entirely accounted for, it cannot be exhausted'.

Roger Bloor

---

[1] Louise Glück, *Disruption, Hesitation, Silence* in *Proofs & Theories* (New York: Ecco, 1994), pp. 77–78.

Hanne Busck-Nielsen looks at a double collection by one of Scandinavia's leading poets. The collections investigate themes of loss, belonging, love, war, terrorism, and the climate crisis of our planet. These two capacious collections are in dialogue with each other, asking fundamental questions through focussing on our senses, and they invite us into the conversation.

Pia Tafdrup, translated by **David McDuff**
The Taste of Steel • The Smell of Snow
Bloodaxe, £12.99

The Taste of Steel and *The Smell of Snow* (published in one volume) arrive in their English translation at a time when Covid-19 has plundered our ability to taste and smell. The collections were published in Danish in 2014 and 2016 respectively, the first of a quintet of our five senses.

The Taste of Steel opens with a broken sugar bowl and the hurt of betrayal – characteristically for Tafdrup the human experience is central; as the poem's title, 'Stages on life's way', intimates, existential questions weave through the collection. Thus, it is no accident that she names one of her philosophical cornerstones, Kierkegaard, at its very opening. In 'Daily Choice', we are confronted with the challenge of choosing life while recognising 'Love is hands that open, everything/may be there or be lost abruptly'. This emotionally intelligent voice contemplates in 'Time and space': 'Life is a continuous state of emergency, / nothing comes back, everything / comes back differently.'

Central to the collection is the poem 'Taste', an extensive, single-sentence list poem (and in the Danish it has a most wonderful rhythm) stretching across different dimensions of reality: sensory, emotional, spiritual, linguistic, and cultural, giving us a taste of Denmark.

Other poems are set further from home in Japan, Paris, and unspecified war zones – 'that's where I obliterate, that's where I'm annihilated.' The 'I' is a personal 'I'; that always takes responsibility; it is inclusive, not confessional. Is it a steely voice? A hardened poet speaking? While steel is indeed a theme underscoring many poems, its cool unyielding heightens the vulnerability and warmth of the human body, as for example in one of several erotic poems – 'Not a voice, not a language / a tongue breaks in, drinks my name.'

In 'Porous border', Tafdrup writes about losing her mother into the pit of dementia; as her mother is losing her memory, the poet simultaneously loses her place in the mother's mind – 'When she asks about what once happened, / I nearly cease to exist, don't know who / is cracking and who is intact'. Belonging ultimately lies in the mind of the beholder.

The Smell of Snow continues the use of synaesthesia to highlight how our sensory perceptions create our experience and memory. However, the intellectual framework of existentialism gives way to an emerging 'simplicity' of being in the breath (this of course, equally being a choice).

The collection's first section, 'Breathe in, breathe out' opens with a poem signalling etymological associations, as well – 'Spirit':

   ... 'while each flake seeks
its casual centre in the world, the snowy sky settles
on the earth, something reaches out across the body's limit,
something exists that's greater than I can grasp, merely sense'.

The poem 'I want to be a tree' further speaks of change – 'be a tree in the park for a while, / share the globe with other trees, rest / in myself, breathe in.' However, alongside this personal journey is alarm over climate change as in 'The end of icebergs', icebergs are 'creatures in a struggle for survival' as the rising sea 'wipes all trace of the ice's history.' Tafdrup responds to the world around her– 'it's not our home, / when someone is killed' – significantly that someone being the young man who opened fire in Copenhagen in 2015 and was shot by the police. Despite, or perhaps because of, the recognition of brutality, of human failure, the poems often return to the emotional cornerstone that is love – 'As long as your fragrance is in the world, / you are in the world'... 'I feel certain / about belonging.'

Throughout these two collections, Pia Tafdrup breathes in the world, tastes its complex flavours. Taste and smell, our pre-verbal senses, are given words, and her poems are 'there between us, we talk together, / understand each other in glimpses, reach into each other's lives'.

Hanne Busck-Nielsen

Reviews in brief

Crossing Lines
An anthology of Immigrant Poetry
Broken Sleep Books, £7.99

This is a stunning book, with poems from twenty-six exciting voices, including Isabelle Baafi, Iulia David, Michelle Penn, Maia Elsner, Nóra Blascók and L.Kiew. It is also a much-needed anthology for our times, reminding the citizens of the UK what we owe to those who choose to make their home here; communities and language risk growing stale without the injection of fresh ideas and viewpoints.

Poets included come from all parts of the world, and their poems startle the pages, touching on many aspects of immigration, physical and metaphorical, and on where the borders of civilisation lie.

Some like Hasan Bamyani are exiles. Bamyani, who once taught in Kabul, uses a formal structure and rhyme scheme in his poems. They are tantalisingly printed in the original Dari,[1] portraying that immigrant poets had a previous existence, and that we are all part of a bigger world. In 'The City I come from', translated by James Attlee, who works closely with Bamyani, 'it is always winter'... 'instead of food and water / our people feed on / bitterness and sorrow.'

Since English is not the first language for many of these poets there are often richly unusual images through the way they use this language. In 'untitled' Christina Lai writes: 'In Chinese, the word for "return" is 回 /one open mouth inside another', and she writes in 'when you have nowhere to return to':

> leave syllables as breadcrumbs
> build a roof over your head
> learn to swallow yourself whole

Sometimes there are hints at shocking things the poets might have experienced. Nóra Blascók writes:

> Cord-cutter
> turned Stanley knife in your hand
> you wonder what yours'll be doing
> age seven. Surviving on a pound
> a day? No way, this is Britain,

Loss is a frequent theme. In 'Goldfinch', Maia Elsner finds herself 'wondering what part of you / I lose each day to another language, another song'.

There is the additional frustration of not being accepted, as Mike Ferguson playfully depicts in 'Immigrant Irony':

---

[1] Dari is the Afghan dialect of Farsi.

There's that sideswipe again, some little Englander telling
me Americans do not understand irony just before claiming

I want my country back.

And the foreignness in finding a new place to call home. 'There are no
names on British doors. No one told you that. / Where you come from, all doors
speak their names.' (Lou Sarabadzic).

Finally, linguistic inventiveness: Amy Evans Bauer, maybe inspired by
Joseph Conrad's penchant for coining words, sobs 'ungrammatically' as 'we are
shaped tonight librarily / by day, exist adverbally'. Staying with language, the
experience of being bi-lingual is summed up Zah Rasul: 'last night I dreamt that /
my tongue split in two'.

This book is a joy to read, and one that needs to be read, furthermore its pages might
resonate with anyone who feels an outsider. The last page of this anthology carries
the words: 'Lay out your unrest'. These poems answer that call.

Simon Maddrell
Queerfella
Rialto, £6

Simon Maddrell's prizewinning pamphlet contains poems about being gay, Manx
and living with HIV. But they are equally poems about living from one's truth and
the difficulties that can result from this. 'The Boy with Green Hair', the poet writes,
'didn't want to be different'. They are poignant poems. In 'All too often', the
narrator arranges a date online but finding he's been blocked is left wondering: 'why
did I say / I'm a poet' or was it 'my / HIV / status?'

In 'Alright really', the narrator's longstanding (now seemingly dead)
friend, an unnamed 'She', tries, somewhat clumsily, to be supportive of the
narrator's homosexuality by flirting with Kamil, the poet's lover, as her way of
showing the poet 'it's alright really'. Difference is othering, and alone is a word that
frequently occurs, yet with a sense of the poet having found peace within himself,
and remaining hopeful, even if nothing lasts. In the short closing, 'The Moon is a
Road I Walk Alone' he writes: 'An intimate road opens in me like a tide.'

Unsurprisingly in a poetry pamphlet exploring relationship, there are
sonnets. The title poem, in a three-stanza block, plays with the Manx sailors'
superstition about bad luck resulting from saying 'rat', and euphemisms used, such
as queerfella – illustrating the island's homophobia. Others are 13-line 'sonnets',
such as 'The Naked Truth', wherein the poet recalls an incident from school when
kids were 'shrieking Quentin / Queer' and 'in a single short breath I knew.'

Death is also a recurrent theme. In 'Three Crows' the poet uses crow
symbolism as he recalls an unsatisfactory meeting between Kamil and the poet's
father, after which 'I slept alone missing you both'. The sadness of not being
accepted is explicit in the penultimate poem, 'Half-Rotten, Half-New,' suggesting
the complexity of the word 'love':

My father smiled
I loved the man who loved
the boy who loved men, even
though he shot me with his bow.

Maddrell's poems are pared back, lyrical and rhythmic, and *Queerfella* is a pamphlet of tender poems with a rawness and honesty that can surely not fail to touch the reader.

Zoe Brigley
Aubade after a French Movie
Broken Sleep Books, £6

Those who think of medieval women as submissive shadowy creatures are in for a sizzling wake up in Zoe Brigley's chapbook. Dedicated to the erotic Welsh poet, Gwerful Mechain, they include the medieval poet's proto-feminist poems, written in forms such as the englyn, the cywydd, and cynghanedd. Unsurprisingly perhaps, Sappho came to mind, for there are relatively few good poems about female desire, sex and the body.

The poet's translations after Gwerful are fresh and audacious, and Brigley's. 'Ode to the Cunt' (Cywydd y cedor) is wittily arranged in two columns, each with a different tone:

how smooth her breasts are: So fuck all the witless men,
how arms in bright sleeves   himpathy poets, & sing
are beautiful, not to mention   a song to the cunt for riches

In her notes, the poet writes that she uses Gwerful's poems as a way of owning a feminine voice in a society where women are still being policed and shamed for owning their desire, and quotes Anais Nin: 'I hate men who are afraid of women's strength'.

The second part of the book contains Brigley's own poems, yet seemingly channel Gwerful's intrepid spirit. The title poem, with its epigraph of Truffaut's '*Tomorrow's film will be an act of love*', is a reminder of how swiftly society judges a woman's actions: '*c'est vraiment dégueulasse.*'[2] The poet writes: 'Being / completely honest / was both the easiest & hardest,' so that even now a woman is still trying to piece 'herself together from snatches / of films'.

These are meaningful, fresh and sometimes funny poems. The chant-like final poem, 'Because this love' journeys us from Wales to take its inspiration from the 'Hymn to Ishtar', written on a 16th-century BC tablet:

because I left wet footprints on the floor;
because they tell me that whores are holy;
because I can help what I am no more than a willow can;

---

[2] That's really disgusting.

These are poems that call for sexuality to be ethically, thoughtfully and erotically revalued as 'one of the most beautiful forms of pleasure that human beings can make with each other'[3]. In *Aubade After a French Movie* Brigley poses this same challenge Gwerful set six hundred years ago with poems that ask: 'what might happen if women were set free?'[4]

G.C. Waldrep
The Earliest Witnesses
Carcanet, £12.99

This is a British debut for G.C. Waldrep, but this professor of English has seven collections and four chapbooks in North America. The title poem opens with a reference to the polyphemus moth, named after the one-eyed Cyclops:

> I am a thing of voice, bent low
> over the voiceless, studying
> it, gauging it against what I once knew

which feels central to the poems of this richly discursive collection: giving voice to what and how we witness things, 'whether the blue you see is the same blue I see'[5]. Waldrep revisits with fresh eyes: 'Let's consult the witnesses you said, / & I nodded.... not realising you were speaking of ourselves.'[6] Other words, besides 'witness', also recur, such as eye, tongue, teeth. 'My eye /(read heart), my soul (read eye)... See what letters I brush with my crude hands.'[7]

God, language, love in its many forms, the body, illness and death are themes being witnessed against a backdrop of landscape, as the narrator walks, sometimes in the US but also in Suffolk, Norfolk, the Malvern Hills, Brecon Beacons, Wales. In '[St Melangell's Day, Eastnor (III)]' he writes: 'We lived in the age of explanations, then. We mistook them for light.'

Throughout, there is a sense of the deeply personal, constantly shifting, subtly, to the universal: 'I am the only remaining witness / I, and the wheat and the mustard, and the scouring sky.'[8]

Waldrep's language is richly imagistic: 'At the banquet, cutlets of meat stewed in chocolate & pomegranate, served in glittering tureens', and another feature of his writing is its musicality. Unsurprising, then, to learn that the poet first trained in classical singing. Intertextuality (eg Simone Weil, Mandelstam, Hildegard) add further richness, making this read at times like a literary walk.

These are poems that read like meditations. The penultimate '(When I was dying it was my mother's job, every few hours or several / times an hour to wake me. She shook me slightly insistently... She called my name.) (And I said, later, yes, belief

---

[3] Zoe Brigley, *Aubade After a French Move* (Broken Sleep, 2020), p. 31.

[4] G.C Waldrep, *The Earliest Witnesses* (Manchester: Carcanet, 2021), p. 79.

[5] Ibid '[Additional Eastnor Poem (IX)]' p. 90.

[6] Ibid 'Only Coerce Yourself Gently, & Show' p. 44.

[7] Ibid 'Hephaestus in Norfolk', p. 72.

[8] Ibid '[Additional Eastnor Poem (I)]' p. 74.

is like that.)'[9] This is a wonderful book that speaks of noticing, reflecting, of spirituality.

Simone Atangana Bekono (trans. David Colmer)
how the first sparks became visible
Emma Press. £6.50

Bekono, from the Netherlands, won the Dutch debut poetry prize for her book-length poem looking at race, gender and agency. The nine sections journey through the narrator's experiences as she seeks to make sense of feeling, in '(IIII)', 'broken disembodied and confused', a 'white Western male's thought experiment'. She aligns herself to her blackness but, 'All black people identify with broken people.' In aphoristic style this recurs throughout the book, eg 'all black people don't exist', and Bekono's use of repetition and free-verse form skilfully portray a mind overtaken by obsessive thoughts: 'i think of black a thousand times a day and try to draw / the word out of me'. The poet is stuck, by 'a door that leads nowhere'.

In the next section the poet goes hunting, and the tone becomes more lyrical. The narrator sees: 'the deer standing still as if to enjoy the last bit of sunlight / I was quivering with weariness and my gun was quivering'. What follows explores that moment of captured time, with its silence and clarity of 'both choices and consequences', deer and narrator united by an 'unmade choice', until:

> she turned towards me, both invitation and challenge
> with all the billions of things happening in the space between us
> that make us merge together
> announcing the moment of ignition
> before the first sparks
> become visible

The seeming inevitability and complicity of hunter and hunted are well-captured, with the aftermath of decisions explored in the next section. 'Yes, give up hope but laugh', she continues. 'All bodies do beautiful and painful things.'

The closing section, with its Rumi epigraph about seeing and recognising the evil in oneself, revives the earlier aphorisms, such as 'all black people identify with drowned people', while suggesting 'deer and I are friends / it is only coincidence that I am the hunter.' The reader is left questioning whether we are drawn to our own self-destruction: 'I feel incomprehensibly attracted to the black water / like us standing on the edge of a cliff / a towering cliff, looking down'.

This is an impressive and thoughtful debut from an original young voice.

---

[9] Ibid '[Carn Goch]' p. 111.

94

Lisa Luxx
fetch your mother's heart
Out-Spoken Press, £10

Lisa Luxx is a queer poet of mixed Syrian-British parentage. This, her debut collection, explores the obsessive love of our wanting, whether romance or revolution, where 'our longing will always be a type of grief'.

Luxx's collection opens in her home in Beirut, as she reflects on seminal events in October: her lesbian lover, a betrayal, a friend's suicide, an attempted murder and revolution on the streets. Soon 'we cannot remember where we hid our great mother's heart'. Mother, here, might be personal or refer to motherland, or possibly to Neuman's book, *The Great Mother*, on the Jungian mother archetype.

'Fetch' in the title is also interesting, its meaning may include: bring forth, achieve, inflict a blow, cause great delight. Perhaps it's all these, and a need to connect to a bigger concept of love. Some poems also have intertextual reference to the ancient Bedouin tragic love story, *Majnun Layla* about desire, and the poet relates a cautionary tale of:

> a mother whose son
> hungered for her love so much,
> he cut her heart out of her chest,[10]

The poems are divided into six 'chapters' with lyricism that stretches language to new limits; they are pared back, in exciting, diverse forms, and with the energy of honesty.

The poet considers her absent Arab father, 'for 28 years I was wearing the features / of a man I didn't know',[11] but ancestral calling is powerful. The poet remembers: ' how this body felt home explode on the edge of Damascus / while I was in bed in Yorkshire'.[12]

In revolutionary times, there can be a sense of becoming inured to violence: 'we're dancing laughing clapping ha dancing when / man beside me pours gasoline on himself // & eats —'[13]

There is also tenderness: 'We are barefoot as new beginnings/washing each other warm'. Later, 'in batroun':

> I said *it's here, between these two rocks that I*
> *feasted with the ghost of my suicide friend, and it's*
> *here that I made love to a Leila I worshipped,*

This is a mesmerising collection and the final poem, 'aka sandcastles in eternal renewal', nods to the repercussions our lives and passions leave behind: 'Everything that falls in orange keeps / searching through its afterlife until it lives again'.

---

[10] Lisa Luxx, *fetch your mother's heart* (London: Out-Spoken Press, 2021), p. 18.
[11] Ibid p. 60.
[12] Ibid p. 59.
[13] Ibid p. 17.

Khairani Barokka
Ultimatum Orangutan
Nine Arches, £9.99

London-based, Jakarta-born Khairani Barokka writes from her Indonesian Minangkabau roots, which has the world's oldest matrilineal culture. This, her second collection, explores the rippling effects of colonial exploitation. The opening poem, 'Sequelae', nods to such lasting results of injury, but equally could refer to the poet's chronic pain, and to how we treat our bodies, including our soul-bodies. This poem ends with a world being left behind: 'You have always known how to tell time by sky.'

The title poem unpacks the shockingly 'twisted phobia' of how the West portrayed chimps in relation to humans, with King Kong 's 'Indonesian roots'. She writes: 'I understand visualchimp language. / I know what KK was trying to say'. Palm oil plantations have destroyed forests, but also 'Orangutans, and so many peoples'.

Barokka's poems are often angry. In Terjaga III she refers to 'theft by romanticised pirates we see on tv. children asking for death.' Her language is fresh. In 'give me a pass' the poet's body is 'a fear-wrapped flesh blanket'. She rails against children being made to 'study English and Western science in tandem with money-goals; in lieu of ancient wisdoms'.

The poem 'Klima(k)tik' is particularly affecting: 'Baring tree trunks chopped dead at the root, we whisper old prayers to survive these shocks and terrors, celsius truths.' which the poet refers to as the 'mapped wounds,' of a body.

Her enjoyably wide range of forms includes specular, anaphora and abcedarian, and Barokka's is a confident assured voice. Sometimes she inserts Indonesian words and references to cultural myths and belief systems, which give the book additional richness; for example, 'tradition in Minangkabau spirituality means everything in its right place'. The poet continues: 'ourselves are not singular but a plurality beyond our comprehension. the nightmares and dreams of other family imprinted from within. and we take them'.

Early on she writes 'i am writing from a drowning ship'[14]and aptly chooses as her line for a golden shovel, 'My poems aren't poetry they're dark words, they sweat, they push one another to get out'[15]. This rings true. They are urgent: they are fresh and powerful poems that stay with the reader.

---

[14] Khairani Barokka, *Ultimatum Orangutan* (Rugby: Nine Arches, 2021), p. 25.
[15] Ibid. 'survivor's remorse, guilt city' takes one line from a poem by the Indonesian political poet Wiji Thukul (as translated by Eliza Vitri Handayani) who has been missing since 1998. p. 68.

Contributors

Vasiliki Albedo's poems have appeared in magazines including *Ambit, Magma, Mslexia, Poetry Salzburg Review, The Morning Star, The Rialto* and *Tears in the Fence*. In 2018 she was commended in the National Poetry competition. She was joint winner in the Live Canon pamphlet competition 2020.

Sharon Ashton graduated in Classics in the 70s, trained as a nurse in the 80s, and graduated in Creative Writing in the 2000s. A published poet and novelist, she retired from nursing to write more, but now finds herself giving Covid vaccines. To read her work visit: sharonashtonpoetry.com

Lizzie Ballagher, having spent all her professional life in editorial and teaching work, now enjoys more time to write. A member of the UK Society of Authors and of the Poetry Society, she lives and works in southern England.

Lerah Mae Barcenilla was born in Manila, Philippines. A writer and poet she grew up in a small province full of magic, tradition and superstition. Currently based in Birmingham, her work touches on topics of the diaspora, memory, mythology and the state of duality. She particularly enjoys breaking apart narrative structures and exploring how words exist on and outside of the page.

Amy Bobeda holds an MFA from Naropa University where she founded the Wisdom Body Collective, an artist collective rooted in the Sacred feminine. Her work can be found in *Humble Pie, Vol. 1 Brooklyn* and elsewhere.

Jonathan Bradley has been writing poetry from an early age. His publications include *Papiliones*, *A Kaleidoscope of Butterflies* and *Sibling Poets*, as well as poems and articles in magazines. His next poetry collection is forthcoming. He has worked as an academic and for an organisation connected with the United Nations.

John Brennan is a British artist whose work centres on emotional and contextual conflict. The fiction and popular culture of his youth continue to influence his painting, across a disparate range of subjects that connect within a single interior world. Brennan has exhibited in many group shows and prizes including Creekside Open, Arte Laguna Prize and Neo Art Prize. He was a finalist in the Contemporary British Painting Prize (2016) and 1st prize winner of the Art Gemini Prize (2015). His work is held in collections in the UK and Germany.

Dorothy Burrows spends her retirement writing and walking on the edge of the North Wessex Downs. Her poems have been published by *The Ekphrastic Review, Another North, Nine Muses Poetry, Words for the Wild* and *Wales Haiku Journal*; another will appear soon in *Spelt Magazine*. Her flash fiction was nominated for *Best Small Fictions 2021*.

Hanne Busck-Nielsen is Danish; her poems have been published by *Interpreter's House, Corbel Stone Press, Albion Beatnik Press, White Rat Press* and *The Poet's House, Oxford.* Her translations of the Danish award-winning poet, Henrik Nordbrandt, have been published in *'POEM, International English Language Quarterly'.* In 2015 she received a Special Commendation in Oxford Brookes University International Poetry Competition.

Diana Cant is a child psychotherapist with an MA in Poetry from Newcastle University and the Poetry School. Her poems have been published in various anthologies, and more recently in *Ink, Sweat and Tears, Brittle Star* and *Finished Creatures.* Her pamphlet, *Student Bodies 1968,* was published last year by Clayhanger Press.

Chrissie Dreier is a mother of three and former teacher who now works for an online educational enterprise. Alongside reading and writing, she enjoys listening to music and playing the drums. She plays in a function band (when not prevented from doing so by a global pandemic).

Katherine Duffy is an Irish poet. Her pamphlet *Talking the Owl Away* (Templar, 2018) won Templar's Iota Shot Award. Two previous collections were published by the Dedalus Press (Ireland). More recent work has appeared in *Poetry Ireland Review, The Blue Nib* and other magazines. Website: www.kateduv.com

Linda Ford is a Derbyshire-based poet and originally comes from a therapeutic background. Her work has appeared in *Reach, Orbis, Diamond Twig* and elsewhere. She has recently completed an MA in Creative Writing with distinction at the Open University. www.lindafordpoet.co.uk

Victoria Gatehouse lives in West Yorkshire and came to poetry in mid-life, after a career in medical research. Her poems have been published in numerous magazines, and she has won the *Ilkley, Otley, PENfro* and *Poetry News* competitions. Victoria's pamphlet *The Mechanics of Love* was published by Smith|Doorstop in 2019.

Amlanjyoti Goswami's recent collection of poems *River Wedding* (Poetrywala) has been widely reviewed. His poetry has been published in journals and anthologies around the world. A Best of the Net nominee, his poems have also appeared on street walls in Christchurch, exhibitions in Johannesburg, an e-gallery in Brighton and buses in Philadelphia. He has read in various places, including New York, Delhi and Boston. He grew up in Guwahati, Assam and lives in Delhi.

Caroline Hammond lives in London and is a founding member of LetterPress Poets. Her poems have appeared in magazines and anthologies including *Ink Sweat and Tears, Under the Radar, Finished Creatures* and *The Emma Press Anthology of Contemporary Gothic Poems.*

Chris Hardy's poems have been widely published in magazines, anthologies and online. He is also a musician, in LiTTLe MACHiNe, performing their settings of well-known poems at literary festivals in the UK and elsewhere. His fourth collection, *Sunshine at the end of the world,* was published by Indigo Dreams.

Rosie Jackson came to poetry late in life but is now widely published. Her books include *The Light Box* (Cultured Llama, 2016), *Two Girls and a Beehive: Poems about Stanley Spencer and Hilda Carline* (Two Rivers Press, 2020) and *Aloneness is a Many-headed Bird,* co-written with Dawn Gorman (Hedgehog Press, 2020). She lives in Devon. www.rosiejackson.org.uk

Bill Jenkinson likes English, French, and German poetry and making poems from pictures, sculptures, photographs, films, or music. He has contributed to exchanges with Bonn poets and projects in Oxford museums, including the Ashmolean, History of Science and Pitt Rivers. He has helped run Oxford Stanza 2 since 2011.

Gurupreet K. Khalsa is a current resident of Mobile, Alabama, having lived previously in Ohio, Washington State, India, New Mexico and California. She received her PhD in Instructional Design from the University of South Alabama. She is a part-time online instructor in graduate education programs.

Seán Kiely recently graduated from Newcastle University with an MA in Writing Poetry. He has been published in *The Echo, Poetry Ireland Review, Honest Ulsterman* and *Bridges*, and has performed at the Kilkenny Arts Festival, the Newcastle Poetry Festival, Cáca Milis Cabaret, and the Coracle Europe Autumn Festival.

Allan Lake is originally from Saskatchewan, and has lived in Vancouver, Cape Breton, Ibiza, Tasmania and Melbourne. Poetry Collection: *Sand in the Sole* (Xlibris, 2014). Lake won Lost Tower Publications (UK) Comp 2017 and Melbourne Spoken Word Poetry Fest 2018 and publication in *New Philosopher* 2020. Chapbook *My Photos of Sicily* (Ginninderra Press 2020).

Emma Lee's publications include *The Significance of a Dress* (Arachne, 2020) and *Ghosts in the Desert* (IDP, 2015). She co-edited *Over Land, Over Sea* (Five Leaves, 2015), is Reviews Editor for *The Blue Nib*, reviews for magazines and blogs at http://emmalee1.wordpress.com. FB: https://www.facebook.com/EmmaLee1. Twitter @Emma_Lee1.

Juliette Lee is a coach, facilitator, podcaster and award-winning speaker for the leading chief executive organisation, Vistage. A former chemical engineer with ICI, she spent 25 years in northern England before returning to her native Scotland. Juliette now lives in South Queensferry and follows her passion for horses and poetry.

Nicole Lee was born in Kuala Lumpur and educated at Malvern and Oxford. She has worked as a banker in Hong Kong and London and now lives in Wandsworth, works in Kew and writes poetry. She has been published in various online journals and long-listed in the National Poetry Competition.

Sara Levy is a Welsh-born poet and freelance proof-reader, studying for a Newcastle University/Poetry School MA in Writing Poetry. Her poems have been shortlisted in the 2020 Oxford Brookes International Poetry and Coast to Coast to Coast competitions, and published in *The Moth, Poetry News, The Alchemy Spoon* and several anthologies.

Sheila Lockhart is retired from social work and lives in the Scottish Highlands. She started writing poetry four years ago after her brother's suicide and has been published in *Northwords Now, Nine Muses Poetry, Twelve Rivers, StAnza Poetry Map of Scotland, Writers' Cafe, Ekphrastic Review* and *Re-Side*.

Jane Lovell is an award-winning British poet whose work focuses on our relationship with the planet and its wildlife. Her latest collection is the prize-winning '*God of Lost Ways*' (Indigo Dreams Press). Jane also writes for *Dark Mountain, Photographers Against Wildlife Crime* and *Elementum Journal*. She lives in Kent and is Writer-in-Residence at Rye Harbour Nature Reserve.

Jennifer A. McGowan took her PhD from the University of Wales. She is a disabled poet and short story writer, started submitting to journals at age five and just kept going. She much prefers the late-fifteenth century to the early twenty-first. Except for indoor plumbing. That can stay.

Peter Mladinic has published three books of poems: *Lost in Lea, Dressed for Winter*, and *Falling Awake in Lovington*, all with the Lea County Museum Press. He lives in Hobbs, New Mexico.

Heather Moulson has been writing poetry since 2016 and has performed regularly in London and Surrey. She has also been interviewed on Soho Radio in 2020. Heather is also a cartoonist, curates a poetry website, and lives in Twickenham with a stroppy black cat whom she constantly draws.

Naomi Murcutt spends most of her time looking after her two young sons in Abingdon, Oxfordshire. Over her lockdown maternity leave, she has rediscovered the joy of writing poetry. She is also an English Teacher and is looking forward to spreading her love of creative writing to her students when she returns to work.

Lorrie Ness is an emerging poet working in Virginia. Her work can be found at *Palette Poetry, THRUSH Poetry Journal, Typishly* and she was a featured poet at *Turtle Island Quarterly* in 2021. In 2020 and 2019 she was nominated for a Best of the Net Award by *Sky Island Journal*.

Kate Noakes is a PhD student at the University of Reading researching contemporary British and American poetry. Her most recent collection is *The Filthy Quiet* (Parthian, 2019). She lives in London where she acts as a trustee for the writer development organisation, Spread the Word. www.boomslangpoetry.blogspot.com

Antoni Ooto is well-known for his abstract expressionist art, and now adds his voice to poetry. Reading and studying the works of many poets has opened another means of self-expression. His early years were spent as a stone mason in the construction industry. Some of those experiences work themselves into his poems.

Ilse Pedler came late to poetry having had a career as a veterinary surgeon. She has had poems published in *Magma, Stand, Strix,* as well as several anthologies. Her pamphlet, *The Dogs That Chase Bicycle Wheels*, won the 2015 Mslexia Pamphlet competition and her first collection is due out with Seren in June.

Mary R. Powell has poems published in *Here/There Poetry, The Letterpress Poets Anthology, Finished Creatures* and in *The Covid Anthology 2020* (Palewell Press): She has an MA in Poetry Writing from The Poetry School/Newcastle University.

Wilfried Schubert, a native of Trier, Germany, has been practising medicine since 1980 and writing poems since 1990. He made his publishing debut in *Denver Quarterly* 54.4 (2020). Work is forthcoming in *Hummingbird: Magazine of the Short Poem, Ethel, EcoTheo Review, Tammy*, and *The Shoutflower*. He and his family live at the eastern edge of Cologne.

Mary Senier is a twenty-six-year-old psychology graduate from the Black Country. Her work tends to experiment with structure, often focusing on ideas of place, capturing snapshots of the ethereality of nature, and identity. She has previously had two poems published by Abergavenny Small Press.

Lesley Sharpe teaches literature and creative writing in London. Her poems have been published in the *Aesthetica Creative Annual, Dragons of the Prime* (Emma Press) and *Finished Creatures #1,* shortlisted for the *London Magazine, Aesthetica* and *Bridport* prizes, and longlisted for *Primers 2* (Nine Arches Press) and Cinnamon Press 2018 Debut Collection Prize. She edits *Heron* magazine for the Katherine Mansfield Society, and co-founded Lodestone Poets.

Oliver Smith is a writer from Cheltenham, UK. He was awarded first place in the BSFS 2019 competition for his poem *Better Living through Witchcraft* and his poem *Lost Palace, Lighted Tracks* was nominated for the 2020 Pushcart Prize. He holds a PhD in Literary and Critical Studies.
https://oliversimonsmithwriter.wordpress.com

Tessa Strickland runs a private psychotherapy practice in Somerset. She also mentors people working in the arts and healing professions. Founder and for 24 years Editor-in-Chief of Barefoot Books Ltd she has written in prose and verse for children and adults. Previous poetry has appeared in *Frogmore Papers, Happenstance Press, Magma, Poetry Ireland Review* and other publications.

Sue B. Walker is Professor Emerita at the University of South Alabama where she taught Creative Writing. She served as Poet Laureate of Alabama from 2003-2012. She has published ten books and is the Editor / Publisher of Negative Capability Press.

Moira Walsh was born in Michigan and has lived on three continents. She is currently based in Germany, where she writes and translates. She became a published poet in 2020, at age 41. Moira is the 2021 Anne-Marie Oomen Fellow at Poetry Forge and a Thomas Lux Scholar at the 2021 Palm Beach Poetry Festival. https://linktr.ee/moira_walsh

Melody Wang currently resides in sunny Southern California with her dear husband. In her free time, she dabbles in piano composition and enjoys hiking, baking, and playing with her dogs.

Geoffrey Winch's poetry was first published in 1992 in his fiftieth year and has since appeared regularly in small press magazines in the UK, US and online. His most recent collection is *Velocities and Drifts of Winds* (Dempsey and Windle, 2020). Also in 2020 he was nominated for the Forward Prize for 'best single poem'.

Sue Wallace-Shaddad's poems have been included in a variety of anthologies and magazines. Her short collection *'A City Waking Up'* was published by Dempsey and Windle, October 2020. Sue has an MA from Newcastle University/ Poetry School London. She writes poetry reviews and is Secretary of Suffolk Poetry Society.

Pat Winslow has published seven collections, most recently, *Kissing Bones* with Templar Poetry. A winner of several notable competitions over the years, she is currently enjoying commissioned collaborations with artists, filmmakers and composers. Pat also works as a storyteller.
www.patwinslow.com and https://thepatwinslow.blogspot.com/

Kate Young lives in Kent. Her poems have appeared in *Nine Muses, Ekphrastic Review, Nitrogen House, Words for the Wild, Poetry on the Lake*, Hedgehog Press and a Scottish Writers Centre chapbook. Kate's work has also featured in the anthologies *Places of Poetry* and *Write Out Loud*.

Submission Guidelines

We welcome submissions of up to three brilliant, unpublished, original poems on the issue's theme through the website during the submission window. You will find full details of how to submit on our website: www.alchemyspoon.org.

We are only able to accept submissions from those over 18.

If you have poems published in the current issue of *The Alchemy Spoon,* then we ask that you wait out one issue before submitting more work.

Simultaneous submissions are permitted but please tell us straightaway if a poem is accepted for publication elsewhere.

We aim for a speedy turn-round and will respond to every submission, but we don't offer individual feedback.

Authors retain all rights. However, if a poem is then published elsewhere, please acknowledge that it first appeared in *The Alchemy Spoon .*

Our submission window for Issue 4 will be open 1st–30th June 2021, the theme for issue 4 is 'Body'.

Submission Guidelines for Essays
If you have an essay on some cutting-edge poetry-related topic, please send it to us during the submission window for consideration +/- 1500 words.

Submission Guidelines for Artwork
We are looking for original artwork to feature on future magazine covers. Portrait-orientated images work best (or images suitable for cropping). Good quality lower resolution images can be sent at the submission stage, but higher res files will be needed (2480 pixels x 3508 pixels) at print stage.

Submission Guidelines for Reviews
If you would like to recommend a poetry collection or submit a review of a collection, then please email us or use the contact form on the website.

Poetry Workshops
The Alchemy Spoon editors offer a one-to-one poetry feedback and workshopping service without prejudice via Zoom or Facetime. All profits from this contribute to the cost of running Clayhanger Press. Please email vanessa.tas@btinternet.com to discuss this.

Printed in Great Britain
by Amazon